PENGUIN PASSNOTES

GCSE Biology: A Book of Revision T

Paul Haddlesey was educated at Bedford College, University of
London, and received his postgraduate Certificate of Education from
the Institute of Education at London University. He now teaches in a
comprehensive school in north London.

PENGUIN PASSNOTES

GCSE Biology
A Book of Revision Tests

PAUL HADDLESEY
ADVISORY EDITOR: STEPHEN COOTE. M.A., PH.D.

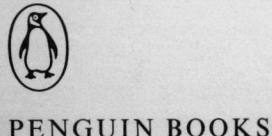

PENGUIN BOOKS

Penguin Books Ltd, Harmondsworth, Middlesex, England
Viking Penguin Inc., 40 West 23rd Street, New York, New York 10010, U.S.A.
Penguin Books Australia Ltd, Ringwood, Victoria, Australia
Penguin Books Canada Ltd, 2801 John Street, Markham, Ontario, Canada L3R 1B4
Penguin Books (N.Z.) Ltd, 182–190 Wairau Road, Auckland 10, New Zealand

First published 1988

Filmset in Monophoto Times
Made and printed in Great Britain by
Richard Clay Ltd, Bungay, Suffolk

Acknowledgements

I would like to thank my wife Jacky for her support during the writing of this book and my two colleagues Mary Reed and Veronica Lynn for their advice and encouragement. I would also like to thank my students at East Barnet School for acting as guinea pigs for all the questions in this book.

Contents

1. How to Use This Book

It is very difficult to sit reading books and notes for any length of time, but answering questions is a way of making the process more interesting and of getting some idea of how much you know. That's what this book is all about. There are several ways you can benefit from using this book properly.

Each chapter is divided into three sections.

Section 1 shows you how to go about answering different types of questions.

In Section 2 you have a chance to try lots of different types of questions. You will use books to do these questions so you will be revising as you work through them. If you have a copy of the *Penguin Passnotes: Biology* book you will not need to spend a lot of time looking up information. You will find that each chapter in this book covers the same sorts of information as the chapter of the same name in the *Passnotes* book.

Section 3 is your opportunity to show off. You are supposed to try these questions without referring to books. It really isn't worth cheating here because nobody knows how you've done except yourself. You should try to do these sections in the time indicated as this will help you to get used to exam conditions.

Marking

At the end of every chapter there are answers to the questions in Sections 2 and 3. The number of marks for each question is also given. With most of the questions it is easy to tell what marks are for what. For example, if you are asked for five labels on a diagram and there are five marks available, there is one mark for each correct label.

Some of them are not so easy to mark and you have to be honest with yourself. For instance, if you have only provided about half of the information that you should have then only give yourself half the marks for that question.

Finally, there is one important point you should remember. This book is not only going to make your revisions more interesting and fruitful, it is also going to make them more fun. Exams are a serious business but don't let them get you too uptight because you will stop thinking clearly. So, if you don't do very well in a particular chapter, or if you don't get merit marks for everything, you should not let it upset you. Just go and do a bit more revision and try again. You'll find that you remember more each time. And when you're tired of serious revision have a go at the puzzles at the end of some of the chapters.

2. The Organization of Life

This chapter is to do with life, and really that is what biology is all about. These questions are based on the information in Chapter 3 of the *Passnotes* book, and what you learn there will give you essential background knowledge to all the other topics in the syllabus.

Section 1

This section contains three long questions, each divided into several parts. The answers are also given so all you have to do is read and, hopefully, understand.

1.

An experiment was carried out to investigate the action of saliva on starch. Six test tubes were taken and to each was added 3 cm^3 of a 1 per cent starch solution. The test tubes were then placed in beakers containing water at different temperatures. Five other test tubes, each containing 1 cm^3 of fresh saliva, were also used, being put into beakers A to E. Figure 2.1 shows how the experiment was set up.

After a few minutes the saliva was added to the starch solutions A to E. No saliva was added to F.

Immediately, a drop of each solution was removed and tested with iodine. This procedure was repeated every minute for 15 minutes.

Results
The results are as follows:

A. Starch test positive after 15 minutes.
B. Starch test negative after 11 minutes.
C. Starch test negative after 6 minutes.

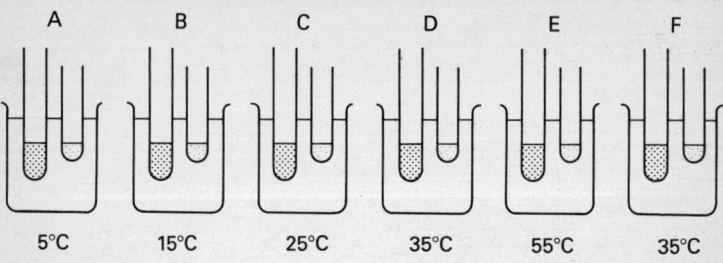

Fig. 2.1

D. Starch test negative after 2 minutes.
E. Starch test positive after 15 minutes.
F. Starch test positive after 15 minutes.

Now come the questions:

QUESTION

Read the method and study the results carefully.

COMMENT

This means what it says. Make sure you understand what was done and WHY before you answer the questions.

(a) What do you think has happened to the starch in tubes B, C, and D?   (2 marks)

The starch has been changed into something else, probably sugars, by something in the saliva.

2 marks for this, so 'gone away' is not enough.

(b) What do you think caused this to happen?   (2 marks)

An enzyme in the saliva (salivary amylase).

1 mark for saying 'enzyme', second mark for knowing which enzyme.

(c) Why do you think the test tubes were left in the water for several minutes before the saliva was added to the starch?   (1 mark)

This allows time for the solutions in the tubes to reach the same temperature as the water in the beakers.

(d) Why was *fresh* saliva used?
(1 mark)

In case there was any change to the enzyme after a certain amount of time.

(e) Why was no saliva added to tube F? (2 marks)

F was a control to show that any changes were due to the saliva and not just to temperatures.

Control experiments are important. You must show the examiner you know why they are important.

(f) How does temperature affect the action of saliva on starch? (3 marks)

The enzyme works fastest at 35 °C. Its action is slower at temperatures above and below this optimum temperature. At very low temperatures the enzyme does not seem to work at all. At very high temperatures the enzyme is denatured.

3 marks for this means that you should put in as much as you can think of, as long as it is relevant to the question. NEVER say that enzymes are KILLED by high temperatures, because they are not alive in the first place.

(g) What do the results tell you about the normal body temperature of humans? (1 mark)

As the enzyme worked best at 35 °C the normal body temperature of humans must be about 35 °C.

(h) If saliva were taken from an animal whose body temperature was 40 °C, would a negative starch test have occurred in tube D in more than 2 minutes or less than 2 minutes? Explain your answer.
(3 marks)

'Explain' means more than a few words. This question requires a bit of thought and understanding. 3 marks for being brilliant.

More than two minutes because
35°C is less than the temperature of
the animal and therefore the
enzyme would work slower.

General comment
The examining boards are very fond of this sort of question because it
tests your understanding of why certain experiments are carried out.
Always make sure you revise your practical work as well as the
theory.

2.

(a) Label the plant cell shown
below (Fig. 2.2).   (9 marks)

Label as many things as you can.
Everything shown on the diagram
is there for a purpose, i.e. for you
to label. Use a ruler to draw label
lines. Label lines must not cross
each other. Label lines should
touch the part of the diagram they
are labelling – note the labelling of
cell wall and cell membrane. If you
are labelling on lined paper, do not
draw your lines along the lines of
the paper as they may not show up
clearly.

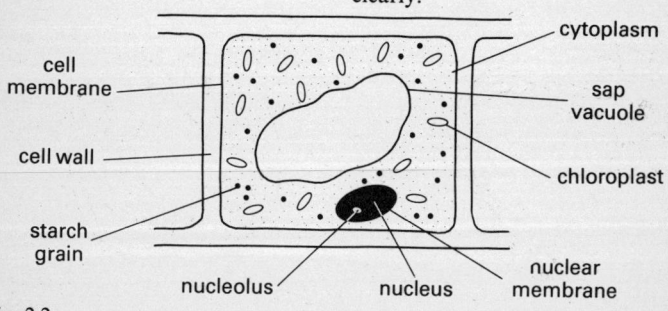

Fig. 2.2.

(b) Draw a large, labelled diagram
of an animal cell (Fig. 2.3).
                         (10 marks)

Note the 'large': small scrappy
diagrams are difficult to see and
annoying to mark. The detail
required depends on your syllabus.
Fig. 2.3 shows the minimum
detail.

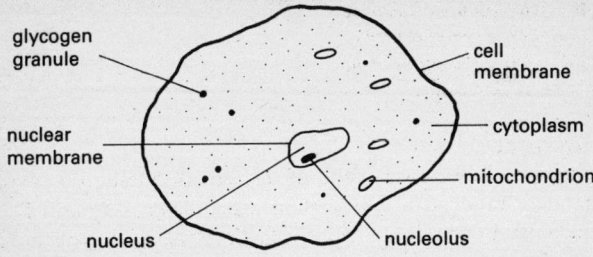

Fig. 2.3.

3.

Cells come in all shapes and sizes. Look at these diagrams of different types of cell.

A. Red blood cells

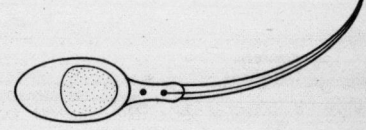

B. Sperm cells

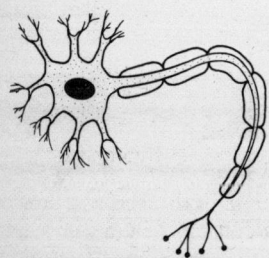

C. Nerve cell

Fig. 2.4

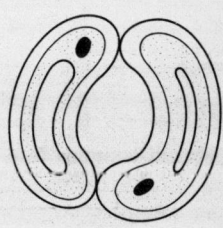

D. Guard cells

Each of these cells has a particular job to do. For each cell, say how its structure is adapted to the job it does. (12 marks)

A. Red blood cell
The biconcave disc shape gives a large surface area for absorption of oxygen. The shape also allows these cells to flow along the blood vessels freely.

B. Sperm cell
The tail provides a way of moving the sperm cell as it has to be able to swim to the ovum to fertilize it. Having the nucleus in the 'head' of the sperm makes it easier for the nucleus to enter the egg cell.

C. Nerve cell
Nerve cells have to carry information (nerve impulses) over long distances. The axon allows the cell to do this.

D. Guard cells
The shape of the guard cells allows them to form a gap (the stoma) between them. The thicker inner wall of each guard cell allows turgor pressure to control the opening and closing of the stoma.

State clearly which cell you are referring to.
You are told that there are 3 marks for each part of the question. This tells you that quite a lot of information is required, as much as you can remember as long as it is relevant. If there were only 1 mark for each part you would know to give less detail and use more time on other questions.

Section 2

Now it's your turn.

This section contains lots of different types of questions. There are marks allocated to each question, adding up to 100 for the whole section. Try to do the questions on your own first, to find out how much you know (or don't know). Then you can work through the questions again using your books and course notes.

I am sure you won't need them but the answers are at the end of the chapter. No cheating.

1. Animal cells do NOT have
   A. a nucleus
   B. a cell membrane

C. chromosomes
D. a cell wall. (1 mark)

2. Which of the following graphs shows the activity of a digestive enzyme as temperature is increased? (1 mark)

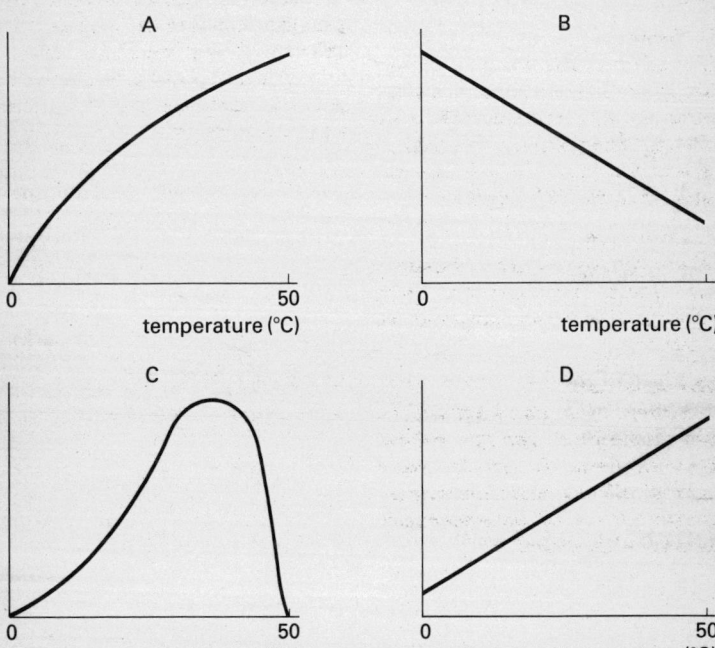

Fig. 2.5

3. The process which produces energy in living organisms is called
   A. respiration
   B. diffusion
   C. breathing
   D. mastication. (1 mark)

4. The cell wall of a plant is made of
   A. starch
   B. cellulose
   C. keratin
   D. protein. (1 mark)

5. A group of cells with similar appearance and function is called
   A. a system
   B. a nematocyst
   C. a tissue
   D. an organ.   (1 mark)

6. Which of the following is in the most logical order?
   A. Cell, tissue, organ, system
   B. Tissue, cell, organ, system
   C. Cell, organ, tissue, system
   D. System, tissue, organ, cell.   (1 mark)

7. A car shows *some* of the characteristics of living things. Which of the
following is NOT shown by a car?
   A. Movement
   B. Reproduction
   C. Nutrition
   D. Excretion.   (1 mark)

8. Which of the following is a test for reducing sugars?
   A. Benedict's
   B. Iodine
   C. Millon's
   D. Biuret.   (1 mark)

9. The biuret test uses which two chemicals apart from the test substance?
   A. Copper sulphate and sodium bicarbonate
   B. Sodium hydroxide and copper sulphate
   C. Sodium hydroxide and potassium permanganate
   D. Sodium chloride and potassium permanganate.   (1 mark)

The following questions (10–13) may contain one or more correct
answers. Use the key below to choose A, B, C, D or E as the correct
answer:
   A. Only answer i is correct (i only)
   B. Answers i and ii are correct (i and ii)
   C. All three answers are correct (i, ii and iii)
   D. Answers ii and iii are correct (ii and iii)
   E. None of the answers are correct (none).

10. Carbohydrates are made up of
    i. carbon, hydrogen and oxygen
    ii. six-carbon sugars
    iii. amino acids.   (1 mark)

11. Proteins
    i. contain carbon, hydrogen, oxygen and nitrogen
    ii. sometimes contain sulphur
    iii. are made up of amino acids.   (1 mark)

12. Enzymes
    i. are made of protein
    ii. are specific to one reaction
    iii. work best at temperatures above 60 °C.   (1 mark)

13. A food sample was tested to see which food types it contained. Benedict's test produced a negative result. Dilute hydrochloric acid was then added to the sample and this mixture was boiled. Sodium carbonate was added and then Benedict's test repeated. This time a positive result was obtained, showing that
    i. non-reducing sugars were present in the food sample
    ii. protein was present
    iii. hydrochloric acid gives a positive result with Benedict's solution.
                                                         (1 mark)

The multiple choice ends here.

14. Copy out the passage below using words from this list to complete it. Use each word once only.

Monosaccharides, fructose, cellulose, glycogen, sugar, oxygen, two, animals, cell, plants, disaccharide, polysaccharides.

Carbohydrates are made of carbon, hydrogen and .... These elements are arranged into .... molecules containing six carbon atoms. These six-carbon sugars are called .... Disaccharides are made up of .... of these, while .... are made up of many. Examples of monosaccharides are glucose and .... Maltose is a ...., starch and .... are polysaccharides. Starch is used by .... as an energy store; .... use glycogen for the same purpose. Another polysaccharide, called .... is used to make the .... walls in plants.   (12 marks)

15. Use the words in this list to complete each sentence below.

Limited, solvent, hydrolysis, polypeptides, amino acids, photosynthesis, respiration, chromosomes, excretion, multicellular.

(a) Plants make their food by ....

(b) A fat molecule can be broken down into glycerol and fatty acids by ....

(c) Growth in animals is different from growth in plants because growth in animals is ....

(d) An organism that is made of many cells is called ....

(e) Proteins are made of chains of ....

(f) Water is known as the universal ....

(g) Removal of waste products from the body is called ....

(h) The mitochondria are the site of .... in the cell.

(i) Hereditary material is found within the ....

(j) Amino acids join together to form ....

(10 marks)

16. Which of the following descriptions refer to a plant cell but NOT to an animal cell (there are more than one and less than six):

    A. contains a nucleus

    B. surrounded by a cell wall

    C. contains chloroplasts

    D. surrounded by a cell membrane

    E. contains cytoplasm

    F. has a large central vacuole?

(2 marks)

17. The following table lists a number of the parts of a cell. Copy out the table, then use ticks and crosses to show which parts are found in plant cells and which are found in animal cells.

Parts of cell	Animal cell	Plant cell
Cell wall		
Cell membrane		
Cytoplasm		
Large central vacuole		
Mitochondria		
Chloroplasts		
Nucleus		
Chromosomes		

(10 marks)

18.

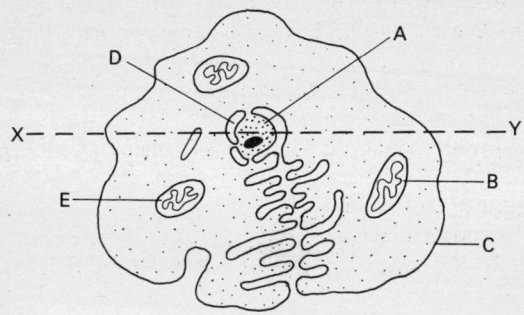

Fig. 2.6

(a) Name the parts labelled A to E in Fig. 2.6.   (5 marks)
(b) What word might you use to describe A, B and C together?
                                                          (1 mark)
(c) What is the function of part E?   (2 marks)
(d) Where would chromosomes be found?   (1 mark)
(e) Is this cell from a plant or an animal?   (1 mark)
(f) To look at the inside of a cell you have to cut it in half. Draw a
    diagram to show what the cell would look like if it had been cut
    along line X–Y.   (3 marks)

19. A rose bush is classified as a living organism.
(a) What seven characteristics must the rose bush show?   (7 marks)
(b) Name two characteristics that could be seen by careful observation
    over a short period of time. Explain what you would expect to see.
                                                          (4 marks)
(c) Name two other characteristics that are not easy to see but could be
    detected by experiments. Describe the experiments you would use.
                                                          (8 marks)

20. Figure 2.7 shows the outlines of a typical animal and a typical plant
cell. Copy these outlines and draw in as much detail as you can, labelling
each structure drawn.   (15 marks)

21. An experiment to test for the presence of protein in a food sample is
described on p. 22. Some of the information has been missed out and it
is up to you to fill in the missing details.

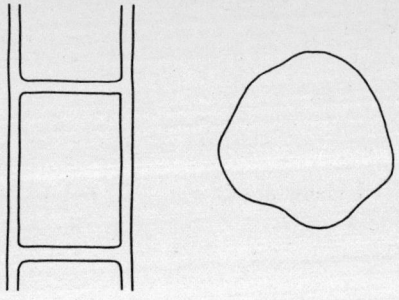

Fig. 2.7

Apparatus
....,   test tube,   sodium hydroxide,
....

Method
1.
2. Add an equal volume of sodium hydroxide.
3.
4. Shake.

Results
The colour of the solution changed to mauve.

Conclusion

(6 marks)

   Now that you have finished this section add up your marks to
get a total out of 100. Questions 18, 19 and 20 are quite hard so if
you got over half marks for these award yourself one merit mark for
each.

Section 3

Definitely no cheating in this bit. There are 10 questions in this section
and you should allow yourself 40 minutes to answer them. After 40
minutes, stop writing and use the answers at the end of the chapter to see
how well you have done.   (40 marks total)

1. Chloroplasts contain
   A. insulin
   B. chlorophyll
   C. chloroform
   D. chromatophores.   (1 mark)

2. Cell membranes are made up of
   A. fat and protein
   B. fat and starch
   C. cellulose
   D. protein and cellulose.   (1 mark)

3. Green plants make their own organic food and are called
   A. phototrophic
   B. automatic
   C. autotrophic
   D. heterotrophic.   (1 mark)

4. The growing regions of plants are called
   A. ribosomes
   B. meriwidows
   C. meristems
   D. stomata.   (1 mark)

5. Which of the following temperatures would human enzymes work
best at?
   A. 37 °C
   B. 42 °C
   C. 33 °C
   D. 28 °C.   (1 mark)

6. Match statements A to E with statements F to J to give complete
sentences.

   A. tissues are   F. have no nucleus
   B. enzymes are   G. the protoplasm
   C. Sudan III is   H. biological catalysts
   D. red blood cells   I. made of cells
   E. The nucleus, cytoplasm and   J. used to test for fat.
      cell membrane are
                                                             (5 marks)

7. Of the seven characteristics of living things which ONE do you think
is most important in each of the following?

A. A person breathing heavily after exercise.

B. A dog chasing a ball.

C. A budgerigar looking in a mirror.

D. A ladybird eating a green fly.

E. A geranium bending towards a window.   (5 marks)

8. An experiment to investigate the action of pepsin (an enzyme that digests protein) was set up as shown in Fig. 2.8. The tubes were kept at 35 °C for 24 hours and then the cubes of egg white were examined.

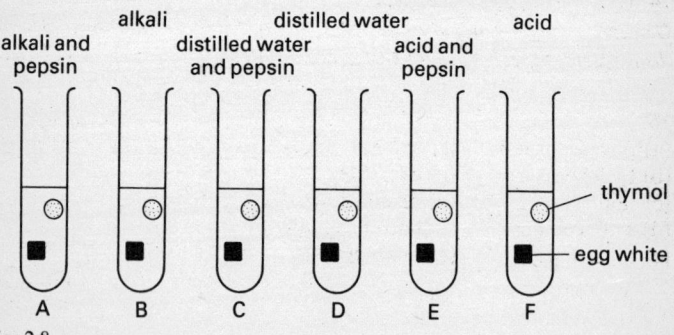

Fig. 2.8

Results

A, B, D and F showed no signs of digestion. The cube in C had been partly digested. The cube in E had been totally digested.

(a) Tubes B, D and F contained no pepsin. What was the purpose of these tubes?   (2 marks)

(b) Why was a crystal of thymol added to each tube?   (1 mark)

(c) Could the thymol have been responsible for the digestion of the protein? Explain your answer.   (2 marks)

(d) Why were all the tubes kept at the same temperature? (2 marks)

(e) What do the results tell you about the optimum conditions for the action of pepsin on protein?   (2 marks)

(f) Where is pepsin found in the human body?   (2 marks)

9. Explain, with the aid of diagrams, how you would investigate the effect of temperature on the digestion of protein by pepsin. (12 marks)

10. When you look at animal tissues through a microscope it is sometimes difficult to see the boundaries between cells. How would you count the number of cells in your sample of tissue?   (2 marks)

If you have finished early, go back and check your answers.

Answers

Section 2

1. D   2. B   3. A   4. B   5. C   6. A   7. B
8. A.   9. B   10. B   11. C   12. B   13. A
(1 mark each)

14. Use the words in this order:
Oxygen, sugar, monosaccharides, two, polysaccharides, fructose, disaccharide, glycogen, plants, animals, cellulose, cell.   (12 marks)

15.
(a) photosynthesis   (f) solvent
(b) hydrolysis   (g) excretion
(c) limited   (h) respiration
(d) multicellular   (i) chromosomes
(e) amino acids   (j) polypeptides.

(10 marks)

16. B, C and F.   (2 marks)

17.

Parts of cell	Animal cell	Plant cell
Cell wall	×	√
Cell membrane	√	√
Cytoplasm	√	√
Large central vacuole	×	√
Mitochondria	√	√
Chloroplasts	×	√
Nucleus	√	√
Chromosomes	√	√

(10 marks)

18.
(a) A. nucleus; B. cytoplasm; C. cell membrane; D. nuclear membrane; E. mitochondrion.   (5 marks)
(b) Protoplasm.   (1 mark)
(c) Making energy by respiration.   (2 marks)
(d) The nucleus.   (1 mark)
(e) An animal.   (1 mark)

(f)

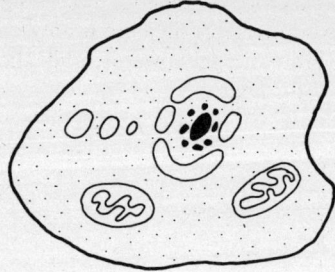

Fig. 2.9   (3 marks)

19.
(a) Movement, feeding (nutrition), respiration, excretion, growth, reproduction and sensitivity.   (7 marks)
(b) *Growth* – an increase in size would be seen. *Reproduction* – over a
period of time a fruit can be seen to be formed from the base of the
flower. This fruit contains seeds which have been formed by reproduction.   (4 marks)
(c) The two characteristics of living things that you could test for here
are nutrition and sensitivity.

Nutrition can be demonstrated by comparing the starch content of
leaves that have been in the light with leaves that have been in the dark.
Leaves that have received light will contain starch and leaves that have
been deprived of light will not contain starch.

The method for testing a leaf for starch is described below:
1. Remove the leaf to be tested from the plant.
2. Place the leaf in boiling water for five minutes to kill the tissue and to
break down the waxy cuticle.
3. Transfer the leaf to boiling ethanol to remove the chlorophyll, thus
making any colour changes easier to see. Ethanol is highly inflammable
so it is heated with hot water to avoid exposure to naked flames.
4. Ethanol hardens the leaf, so put it back into boiling water for a few
seconds to soften it.
5. Put the leaf on a suitable surface, usually a white tile, and cover it
with iodine solution.
6. After one minute rinse off the iodine and note the appearance of the
leaf. If starch is present the iodine will react with it to give a blue-black
colour. If the iodine remains brown there is no starch present.

Sensitivity can be demonstrated by showing that the plant will grow
towards light from one direction.

In this experiment, one group of seedlings receives light from all directions while another group receives light from only one direction. The first group are seen to grow straight upwards, while the second group of seedlings grow towards the light.   (8 marks)

20.

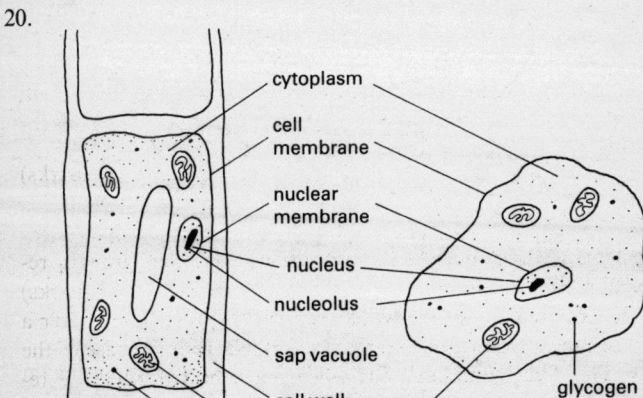

Fig. 2.10

(15 marks)

21.

Apparatus   Food sample and copper sulphate.
Method   1. Place the food sample in a test tube. 3. Add one or two drops of copper sulphate solution.
Conclusion   The food sample contained protein.   (5 marks)

Section 3

1. B   2. A   3. C   4. C   5. A   (1 mark each)
6.
A with I, B with H, C with J, D with F, E with G.   (5 marks)

7.
A. excretion or respiration
B. movement or sensitivity
C. sensitivity

D. feeding

E. sensitivity.   (5 marks)

8.

(a) Tubes B, D and F were used as controls to show that the results were due only to the action of pepsin.   (2 marks)

(b) The thymol was added to kill any bacteria which might have digested the protein.   (1 mark)

(c) The thymol could not have caused the results because thymol was present in the controls where there was no digestion.   (2 marks)

(d) Enzymes are affected by temperature as well as by pH.   (2 marks)

(e) The experiment shows that pepsin works best in acid conditions.

(2 marks)

(f) Pepsin is found in the stomach (only 1 mark if you just said 'digestive system').   (2 marks)

9. This experiment will be very similar to the previous one. The differences are that you would use acid conditions with pepsin at a range of temperatures. Your controls will not contain pepsin. For 12 marks this must be written out fully, with a diagram.   (12 marks)

10. The cells could be counted by counting the number of nuclei present, as there is only one nucleus in each cell.   (2 marks)

3. Movement of Substances Into and Out of Cells

This chapter contains questions about some of the most vital processes that go on in living organisms. So, although it is a short chapter, it is very important that you understand its contents. As you work through the rest of the book you will find that you need to understand diffusion and osmosis to be able to answer other questions.

Section 1

As before, all the work is done for you in this section.

1.

An experiment using half-potatoes with cavities cut in them was set up as shown in Fig. 3.1.

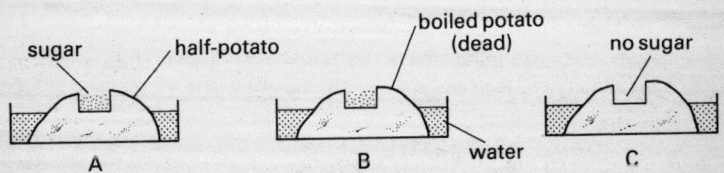

Fig. 3.1.

The apparatus was left for 24 hours and the results noted.

Results
The results are as follows:
  A. The water has risen to the top of the cavity.
  B. There was no water in the cavity.
  C. There was no water in the cavity.

QUESTION

COMMENT

(a) By what process did water rise in A? (1 mark)

1 mark, so brief answer only.

Osmosis

(b) Why did this process occur? (3 marks)

Take this step by step so that you get in as much detail as possible. You would get some marks for just saying that water was drawn in from the petri dish. If you can remember words like hypertonic use them.

The sugar in the cavity created a strong solution so that water from the potato cells moved into the cavity by osmosis. As water was drawn out of the cells, so more water entered the potato from the petri dish.

(c) Why did no water enter B? (1 mark)

The potato tissues were dead in B.

The results tell you this so you should be able to work it out.

(d) What does this tell you about selectively permeable membranes in potatoes? (1 mark)

The membranes have to be alive to allow the passage of water.

Again, this answer follows from the results.

(e) Why did no water rise in C? (2 marks)

There was no sugar in the cavity of C to create a strong solution, so no water was drawn into the cavity by osmosis.

You know this because the presence or absence of sugar is the only difference between A and C.

Section 2

Right then, have a go at this lot.

1. Use the words in the list to complete the following passage:

Gradient, isotonic, lower, high, permeable, hypertonic, weak, hypotonic, strong, cell membrane.

Substances diffuse from an area of .... concentration to an area of .... concentration. The difference in concentration is called a diffusion .... Osmosis is a special sort of diffusion, involving the movement of water across a selectively .... membrane. An example of such a membrane is the .... In osmosis, water moves from a .... solution to a .... solution. The weaker solution is called ...., the stronger solution is called .... Solutions of equal concentration are .... (10 marks)

2. The strength of a solution can be related to its
    A. diffusion pressure deficit
    B. osmotic pressure
    C. active transport
    D. turgor pressure. (1 mark)

3. In Fig. 3.2, which cell is plasmolysed? (1 mark)

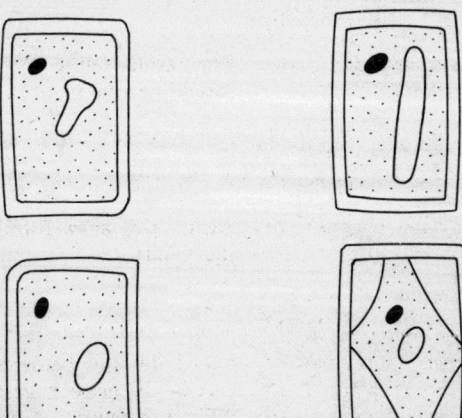

Fig. 3.2.

4. Which of these is an example of active transport?
    A. Movement of oxygen from the lungs to the blood.
    B. Movement of carbon dioxide from the blood to air in the lungs.
    C. Uptake of mineral salts by root hairs.
    D. Movement of oxygen from tissue fluids to cells. (1 mark)

5. Look at Fig. 3.3 and answer the questions.

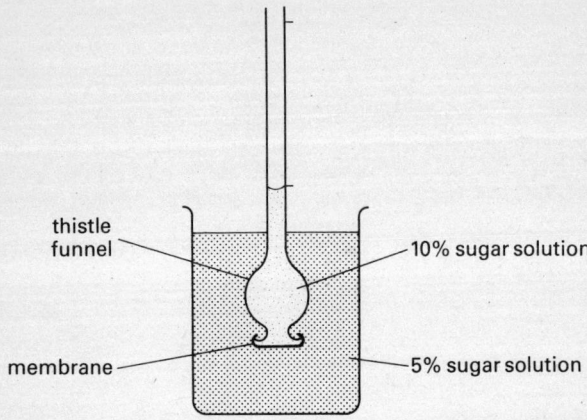

Fig. 3.3.

When the apparatus was left for a while the level of the sugar solution in the funnel rose from A to B.

(a) Why does the level rise in the thistle funnel?   (2 marks)
(b) What sort of membrane is stretched across the mouth of the thistle funnel?   (1 mark)
(c) Would the fluid level in the funnel rise indefinitely or would it stop eventually? Explain your answer.   (4 marks)

6. An experiment was set up as shown in Fig. 3.4. After a while the starch solution turned a blue-black colour.

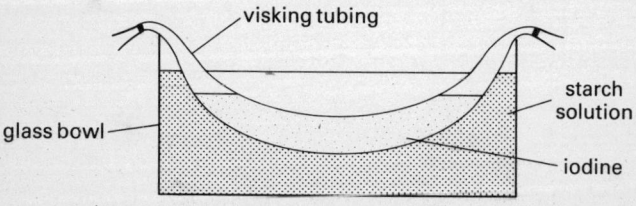

Fig. 3.4.

(a) What happens when iodine is added to starch?   (1 mark)
(b) Why did the starch solution turn a blue-black colour?   (1 mark)

(c) What process has occurred?   (1 mark)

(d) The iodine in the visking tubing did not change colour? What does this tell you about visking tubing?   (2 marks)

There are 25 marks for Section 2. How well did you do? If you got over 15 you have done well. Give yourself 1 merit mark for 20 or more.

Section 3

Allow yourself 30 minutes for this section. There are 20 marks altogether.

1. Figure 3.5 shows what happens to a plant cell placed in water.

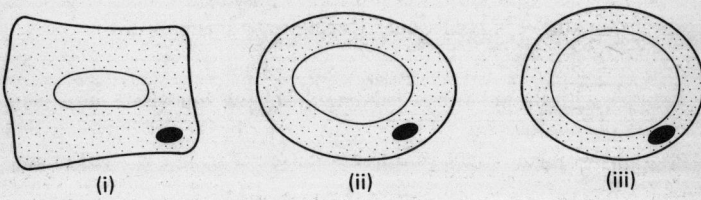

(i)   (ii)   (iii)

Fig. 3.5.

(a) At stage (iii) the cell is
   A. turgid
   B. morbid
   C. rigid
   D. putrid.   (1 mark)

(b) In relation to the water outside the cell, the cytoplasm in the cell is
   A. isotonic
   B. hypotonic
   C. ginandtonic
   D. hypertonic.   (1 mark)

2. Carbon dioxide in the blood moves into the lungs by
   A. ultrafiltration
   B. active transport
   C. diffusion
   D. osmosis.   (1 mark)

3.

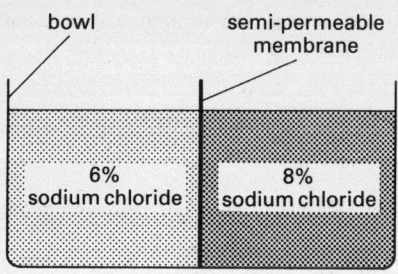

Fig. 3.6.

In Fig. 3.6 there is a movement of water within the bowl. Explain which way the water would move and why. (3 marks)

4. When lettuce goes limp it is sometimes possible to make it go firm again by soaking it in cold water. Explain why this happens.

(2 marks)

5. Explain, with the aid of labelled diagrams, how you would investigate the effects of osmosis on red blood cells. Describe the results you would expect and why you might get these results. (12 marks)

If you finish early, go back and check your answers.

Now mark your answers to see how well you have done. Question 5 is difficult to mark: see how much detail you got in your answer and give yourself a proportion of the 12 marks available.

Answers

Section 2

1. Use the words in this order:
high, lower, gradient, permeable, cell membrane, weak, strong, hypotonic, hypertonic, isotonic. (10 marks)

2. B   3. D   4. C   (1 mark each)

5.

(a) Water moves into the funnel by osmosis because the funnel contains a stronger solution. (1 mark)

(b) A semi-permeable (or selectively permeable) membrane. (1 mark)

(c) The level would stop rising because the water entering the funnel would dilute the sugar solution until it was the same concentration as that in the beaker.   (4 marks)

6.
(a) A blue-black colour is formed.   (1 mark)
(b) Iodine had come into contact with the starch.   (1 mark)
(c) Diffusion.   (1 mark)
(d) Visking tubing allows iodine to pass through but not starch.
                                                                        (2 marks)

Section 3

1. (a) A   (b) D   2. C   (1 mark each)

3. The 8 per cent solution is stronger than the 6 per cent solution so water moves from the 6 per cent solution to the 8 per cent solution until both have reached the same concentration.   (3 marks)

4. The cytoplasm in the lettuce cells is a stronger solution than the water. Therefore water moves into the cells by osmosis, making them turgid so that the lettuce becomes firm again.   (2 marks)

5.
Method
Take two test tubes, one containing distilled water (A) and the other containing a strong salt solution (B).

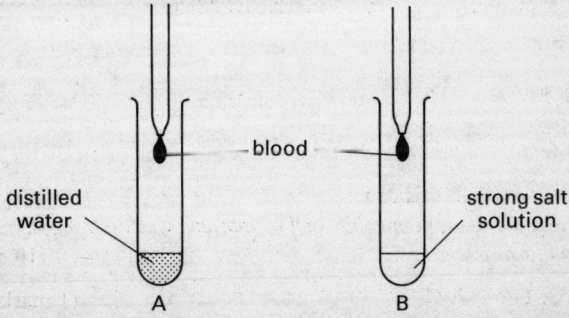

Fig. 3.7.

To each tube add a drop of fresh blood and shake the tubes to mix the contents. Use a clean teat pipette or glass rod to transfer a drop of each solution to a microscope slide. Examine the blood cells from A and B under a microscope, comparing their appearance with a sample of un-treated blood.

Results

The blood cells from tube A would have burst. This is because their cytoplasm is a stronger solution than distilled water, so water enters them by osmosis. Eventually they become so full of water that the cell membrane breaks.

The blood cells from B would have lost water and become wrinkled in appearance. This is because the salt solution is hypertonic to the cyto-plasm so that water moves out of the cells by osmosis.   (12 marks)

4. Feeding (Nutrition)

Over the years many of my pupils have complained that they find plants boring and prefer to concentrate on animal biology. Plants, however, are very important to all of us because of their ability to make food by photosynthesis. So biologists must know about photosynthesis and examiners will check that you know. This makes it especially important to you.

Section 1

1.

The table below shows the results of an experiment to investigate the relationship between the concentration of glucose in the small intestine and the rate of uptake of glucose into the blood.

Percentage concentration of glucose	Rate of uptake (units per minute)
1	30
2	38
3	41
4	45
5	50
6	54
7	60
8	70
9	80
10	100

QUESTION

(a) Draw a graph to show the relationship between glucose concentration and rate of uptake.

(5 marks)

COMMENT

This means a line graph NOT a histogram or bar chart.

Try to join the lines in a smooth curve rather than straight lines between points. Note that the axes start at 0.

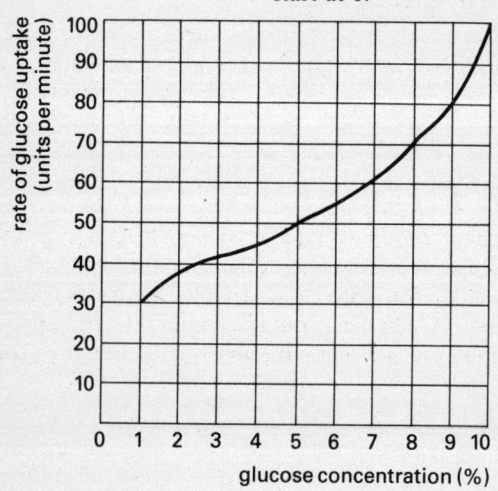

Fig. 4.1.

(b) What would be a more correct word for 'uptake'?   (1 mark)

This means more correct biologically.

Absorption

(c) What is the rate of uptake of glucose at a concentration of 8.5%?   (1 mark)

If you have drawn the graph correctly you can just read off the answer (easy eh?)

75 units per minute

Do not just write '75' – it could mean 75 elephants – always specify units.

(d) If a 4% solution of glucose contains 60 mg (milligrams) of glucose, how much would there be in a 6% glucose solution?

(2 marks)

Simple arithmetic, but a lot of people panic with numbers instead of thinking in steps.

4% = 60 mg
1% = 60 ÷ 4 = 15 mg
6% = 15 × 6 = 90 mg
Hence:
90 mg in 6% solution

Show your working in case you make a silly mistake.

(e) Name an enzyme involved in the digestion of carbohydrate.
                        (1 mark)

Salivary amylase

Other possibilities would be pancreatic amylase, maltase, lactase, sucrase, cellulase.

2.

Sunlight is made up of light of different wavelengths, each of which is a different colour. When sunlight shines on a red football, red light is reflected from the ball while the other colours are absorbed by the ball. This reflected red light enters our eyes so that the ball appears red.

The graph in Fig. 4.2 shows the absorption of light by chlorophyll.

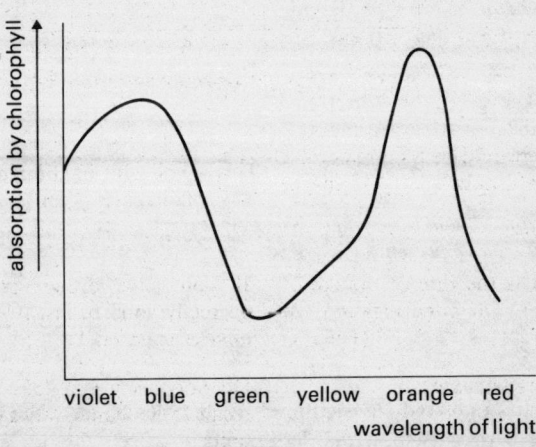

Fig. 4.2

(a) What colour is absorbed most by chlorophyll?   (1 mark)

This answer can be read off from the graph.

Orange

(b) What colour is absorbed least by chlorophyll?   (1 mark)

Green

(c) Why does chlorophyll appear green?   (2 marks)

Now you can see why you were given the information at the beginning of the question. Less green is absorbed than other colours; therefore more green is reflected.

Green light is reflected from chlorophyll, so this green light enters our eyes, making it appear green.

(*d*) *What do plants use chlorophyll for?*   (*1 mark*)

Photosynthesis

Try to spell it right.

(e) What would happen to a plant that had only green light shining on it?   (2 marks)

If you know why plants photosynthesize you know that the plant would die if it could not.

It would be unable to photosynthesize and would therefore die.

(f) Why do leaves often appear to be a darker green on top than underneath?   (3 marks)

The top of the leaf receives more light, so the cells on top contain more chlorophyll and hence there is more green colour present.

This takes a bit of thought about why plants are green and what chlorophyll does.

Section 2

1. Canadian pondweed (*Elodea*) gives off bubbles of gas when exposed to light. Experiments show that light intensity affects the rate at which the gas is given off. The results of such an experiment are given in the table on p. 41.

(a) Draw a graph to show the relationship between light intensity and the rate of gas production.   (5 marks)

(b) What gas is produced by the *Elodea*?   (1 mark)

Light intensity (units)	Bubbles per minute
0	0
50	5
100	9
150	13
200	15
250	17
300	19
350	20
400	20
450	20

(c) By what process is this gas formed?   (1 mark)

(d) Why does gas production level off?   (5 marks)

2. Figure 4.3 shows a section of leaf.

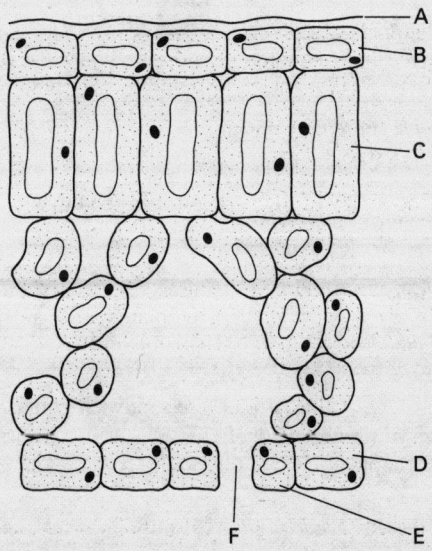

Fig. 4.3.

(a) Name the parts labelled A–F   (6 marks)

(b) Which structure would contain the most chloroplasts?   (1 mark)

(c) Draw a large, labelled diagram to show how the chloroplasts would be arranged in ONE cell receiving dim light from above.

    (3 marks)

(d) If the leaf were in bright sunlight what gas would diffuse into the leaf through F?   (1 mark)

(e) Give a balanced equation for photosynthesis.   (1 mark)

3. The pie charts below show the proportions of the main food types in bread, butter and cheese.

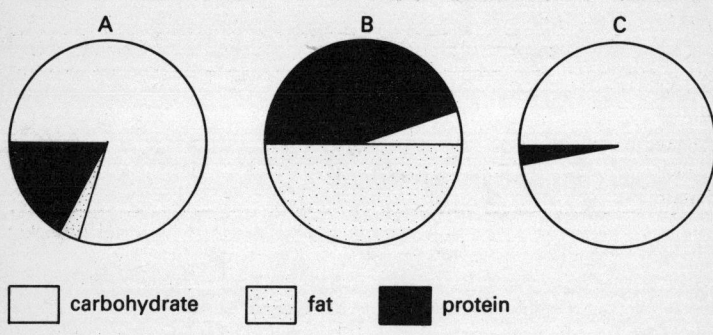

| carbohydrate | fat | protein |

Fig. 4.4.

(a) Which diagram represents which food?   (3 marks)

The energy values of these foods are given in the table:

Food	Energy value kJ/g (kilojoules per gram)
Bread	10·6
Butter	31·2
Cheese	17·3

(b) What is the energy value of a cheese sandwich containing 100 g of bread, 3 g of butter and 10 g of cheese?   (3 marks)

(c) What would happen if you put iodine on bread? Explain your answer.   (2 marks)

4.

(a) Match the illness with the vitamins:

Vitamins lacking	Illness
A. A	E. scurvy
B. B_1	F. beri beri
C. C	G. rickets
D. D	H. poor night vision.

(4 marks)

(b) Why are British sailors sometimes called 'limeys' when they are abroad? (2 marks)

(c) Why are carrots supposed to help you see in the dark? (2 marks)

5. Using ticks and crosses to indicate positive or negative results, complete the table below.

Food	Test			
	Starch	Benedict's	Biuret	Grease spot
Apple				
Bread				
Chewed bread				
Butter				
Potato				

(10 marks)

6.

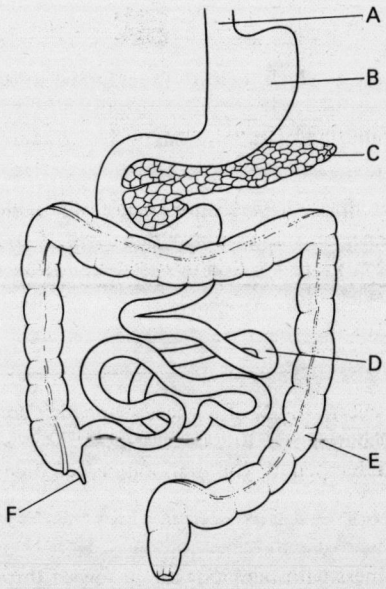

Fig. 4.5.

(a) Name the parts labelled A–F. (6 marks)

(b) In which part would you expect to find pepsin? (1 mark)

(c) Where does absorption take place? (1 mark)

(d) How is the internal surface area of D increased?   (1 mark)
(e) Which part would be much larger in a rabbit?   (1 mark)

7.
(a) Is the skull shown in Fig. 4.6 that of a herbivore or of a carnivore?
        (1 mark)

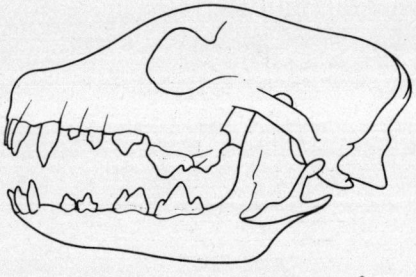

Fig. 4.6.

(b) State two ways in which its teeth are adapted to its diet.

        (4 marks)

(c) Make a large, labelled diagram to show the structure of a mammalian
    tooth.   (5 marks)

When you have finished this section, mark your answers to get a total
out of 70. If you get over 45 you have done well, if you get less than 45
you should do some more work on this section. For over 50 give yourself
1 merit mark; 2 merits for over 60.

Section 3

Allow yourself 30 minutes for this section, there are 30 marks to
    get.

1. Figure 4.7 represents a cross-section of a villus.
(a) Would fatty acids be absorbed into A or B?   (1 mark)
(b) Name two other substances that are absorbed through the villi.

        (2 marks)

(c) How do the villi increase the efficiency of absorption in the small
    intestine?   (1 mark)
(d) Where is food that enters A taken to from the small intestine?

        (2 marks)

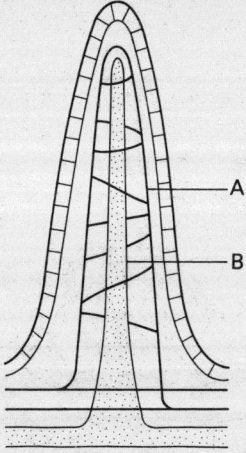

Fig. 4.7.

2.
(a) Draw a large, labelled diagram to show how food is moved along the alimentary canal by peristalsis.   (2 marks)
(b) Name two parts of the alimentary canal where peristalsis occurs.
                                                              (2 marks)

3. Many years ago a scientist named Van Helmont carried out an experiment on how plants feed. He planted a shoot in a pot and then covered the pot so that only water could get into the soil. After 5 years he weighed the plant and the soil and compared these weights with the original weights. His results are summarized in Fig. 4.8.
(a) Van Helmont dried the soil before each weighing. Why did he do this?   (2 marks)
(b) Where did the extra weight of the tree come from?   (2 marks)
(c) What accounts for the small loss of weight from the soil?
                                                              (1 mark)

4. Describe an experiment that would demonstrate the need for carbon dioxide in photosynthesis. Use labelled diagrams where necessary.
                                                              (15 marks)

Now go back and add up your marks. Over 15 is good, over 25 is brilliant (but don't get big-headed).

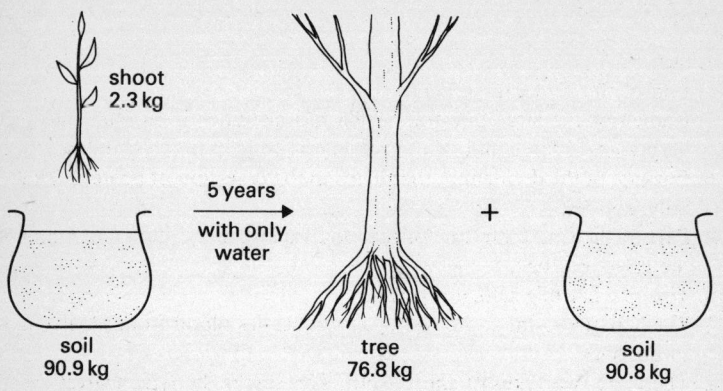

Fig. 4.8.

Crossword

Now that you've got this far you deserve a bit of fun (educational fun of course). Have a go at this crossword.

Fig. 4.9.

Clues

Across

1. End of the alimentary canal.
2. Branch of the large intestine which has no function in man but in herbivores is large and contains bacteria to help digest cellulose.
6. Enzyme in the duodenum that helps in the digestion of proteins and polypeptides.
8. Part of the small intestine of mammals between the duodenum and the large intestine.
10. This is what bile salts do to fats.
11. The hepatic portal .... carries blood from the ileum to the liver.
12. There are two types of cheek teeth. This one is the type nearest the front of the mouth.
16. Some herbivores have this instead of canine teeth.
18. This is one of the pores found on the surface of leaves, mainly on the underside.
19. In a dog this would be pointed but in a sheep it would be flattened.

Down

1. Most plants are said to be this because they make their own organic food from simple inorganic chemicals.
3. There are two types of this in leaves, spongy and palisade.
4. One of the many functions of this organ is bile formation.
5. These are found on the inner lining of the ileum where they increase the surface area for absorption.
7. Foods are moved around in plants in this tissue.
9. Leaves have an upper and a lower of this.
13. This is a polite word for the removal of faeces from the body.
14. This enzyme, which is involved in the digestion of fats, is found in the pancreatic juice.
15. During the .... reaction, chlorophyll traps light energy and converts it to chemical energy.
17. It is because of this that we enjoy eating.

Answers

Section 2

1.
(a)

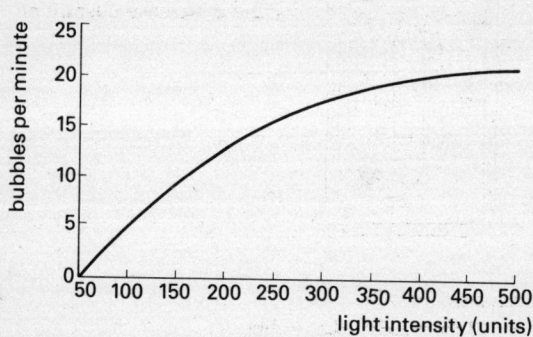

Fig. 4.10.   (5 marks)

(b) Oxygen.   (1 mark)
(c) Photosynthesis.   (1 mark)
(d) The rate of photosynthesis is affected by more than just light intensity. For example, there may not be enough carbon dioxide for a higher rate or the temperature may not be high enough. As the products of photosynthesis build up the reactions slow down. Also there are a limited number of chloroplasts available. Any or all of these limiting factors could be responsible for the levelling off.

(5 marks)

2.
(a) A. cuticle
    B. upper epidermis
    C. palisade cell
    D. lower epidermis
    E. guard cell
    F. stoma.   (6 marks)
(b) C   (1 mark)

(c)

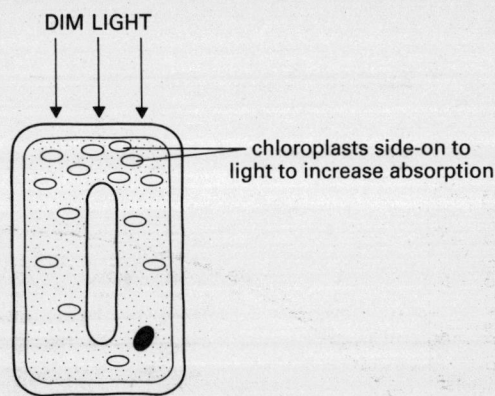

DIM LIGHT

chloroplasts side-on to light to increase absorption

Fig. 4.11.   (3 marks)

(d) Carbon dioxide   (1 mark)

(e) $6CO_2 + 6H_2O \rightarrow C_6H_{12}O_6 + 6O_2$
    $6CO_2 + 12H_2O \rightarrow C_6H_{12}O_6 + 6O_2 + 6H_2O$ (1 mark)

3.

(a) A. bread
    B. cheese
    C. butter.   (3 marks)

(b) Bread $10.6 \times 100 = 1060.0$ kJ
    Butter $31.2 \times 3 = 93.6$ kJ
    Cheese $17.3 \times 10 = 173.0$ kJ

    $\overline{}$

    1326.6 kJ

    Energy value of
    sandwich $- 1326.6$ kJ   (3 marks)

(c) The starch in the bread would react with the iodine to give a blue-black colour.   (2 marks)

4.

(a) A with H, B with F, C with E, D with G.   (4 marks)

(b) British sailors used to eat limes which contain vitamin C to prevent scurvy.   (2 marks)

(c) Carrots contain vitamin A, which is used by the light sensitive cells in the retina to react to light. The presence of vitamin A therefore helps night vision.   (2 marks)

5.

Food	Test			
	Starch	Benedict's	Biuret	Grease spot
Apple	×	√	√	×
Bread	√	×	√	√
Chewed bread	√	√	√	√
Butter	×	×	√	√
Potato	√	×	√	×

(10 marks)

6.
(a) A. oesophagus
    B. stomach
    C. pancreas
    D. small intestine
    E. large intestine
    F. appendix.   (6 marks)
(b) B (stomach).   (1 mark)
(c) D (small intestine).   (1 mark)
(d) By the presence of villi.   (1 mark)
(e) F (appendix).   (1 mark)

7.
(a) Carnivore.   (1 mark)
(b) Any two of these:
    (i) Pointed incisors for tearing meat from bone.
    (ii) Large pointed canines for gripping and killing.
    (iii) Premolars and molars are shaped for cutting through flesh with
         a scissors action or for crunching bones.   (4 marks)

(c)

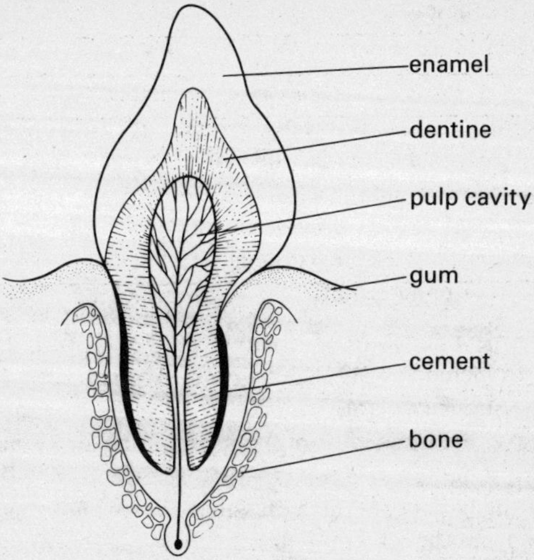

enamel

dentine

pulp cavity

gum

cement

bone

Fig. 4.12.   (5 marks)

Section 3

1.
(a) **B**   (1 mark)
(b) Any two of these:
    amino acids, monosaccharides, vitamins, minerals.   (2 marks)
(c) By increasing the surface area over which absorption can take
    place.   (1 mark)
(d) The liver via the hepatic portal vein.   (2 marks)

2.
(a)

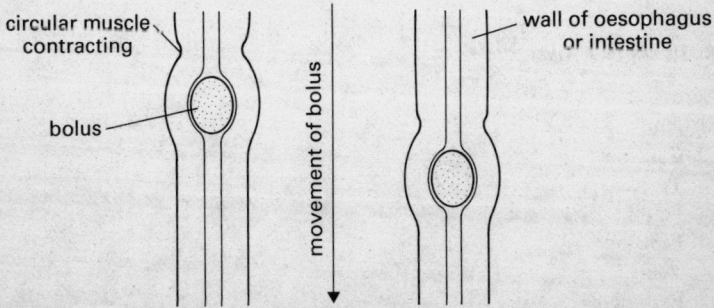

circular muscle contracting

wall of oesophagus or intestine

bolus

movement of bolus

Fig. 4.13.   (2 marks)

(b) Any two of these:
oesophagus, small intestine, large intestine.   (2 marks)

3.

(a) The amount of water in the soil would vary because the plant was watered regularly. Drying the soil allows a direct comparison between the two weights.   (2 marks)

(b) Originally from carbon dioxide in the air which was changed into larger molecules by photosynthesis.   (2 marks)

(c) Absorption of mineral salts.   (1 mark)

4. This experiment is described briefly here. To get your 15 marks you would have to include a GOOD diagram, labelled fully.

  (i) Use a destarched plant.

 (ii) Two leaves are isolated from the surrounding air by enclosing them in flasks

(iii) One of the flasks contains potassium hydroxide to remove carbon dioxide from the air in the flask.

 (iv) The other flask is a control.

  (v) The plant is left in daylight long enough for starch to be made in the control leaf.

 (vi) The leaves must be fixed by boiling and the chlorophyll must be removed before testing.

(vii) Add iodine to test for starch.

(viii) A blue-black colour indicates the presence of starch.

 (ix) The presence of starch in the control leaf indicates that photosynthesis has taken place.

  (x) Lack of starch in the leaf starved of carbon dioxide shows that photosynthesis does not occur in the absence of carbon dioxide.

          (15 marks)

Answers to Crossword

Across

 1. Anus
 2. Caecum
 6. Trypsin
 8. Ileum
10. Emulsify
11. Vein
12. Premolar
16. Diastema

18. Stoma
19. Incisor

Down
  1. Autotrophic
  3. Mesophyll
  4. Liver
  5. Villi
  7. Phloem
  9. Epidermis
13. Egestion
14. Lipase
15. Light
17. Taste

5. Respiration, Gas Exchange and Breathing

Respiration, gas exchange and breathing are terms that are often used wrongly. They each have a different meaning so make sure you are clear what each means. Be sure, also, that you understand the relationship between respiration and photosynthesis.

These questions will help you to clarify the situation. Have fun.

Section 1

1.

The apparatus in Fig. 5.1 shows an experiment that you may have carried out in your practical lessons.

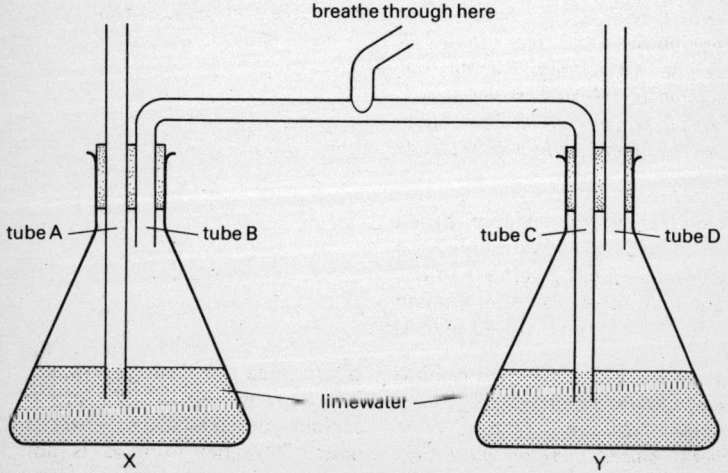

breathe through here

tube A — tube B   tube C — tube D

— limewater —

X   Y

Fig. 5.1.

QUESTION

COMMENT

(a) If you were to breathe in, through which tube would air enter the apparatus? (1 mark)

If you are familiar with this experiment the answer is easy. If not, you have to work it out. Remember you would not be expected to suck up limewater in an experiment.

Tube A

(b) Through which tube does air leave the apparatus when you exhale? (1 mark)

If you can't remember what exhale means, the fact that air *leaves* the apparatus gives you a clue.

Tube D

(c) In which flask does the limewater go cloudy first? (1 mark)

This must be the flask which receives exhaled air – there is more carbon dioxide (CO_2) in exhaled air.

Flask Y

(d) Explain your answer to (c). (3 marks)

Limewater goes cloudy when in contact with CO_2. Exhaled air contains more CO_2 than inhaled air because CO_2 formed from respiration is excreted in the breath. Flask Y receives exhaled air; therefore the limewater in it goes cloudy first.

You must show that you know where the CO_2 comes from.

(e) If this experiment were carried out immediately after exercise the limewater would go cloudy in less time than before exercise. Explain this. (3 marks)

When energy is made by respiration, CO_2 is produced as a waste product. During exercise, more energy is used, therefore more CO_2 is produced. Consequently, after exercise there is more CO_2 being excreted in exhaled breath.

If you think this through logically it is very easy (honest!) Be sure to explain your reasoning, 'There is more CO_2 after exercise' is not enough.

2.

Figure 5.2. shows a model that demonstrates how we inhale. When the sheet of rubber is pulled down, the balloons inflate.

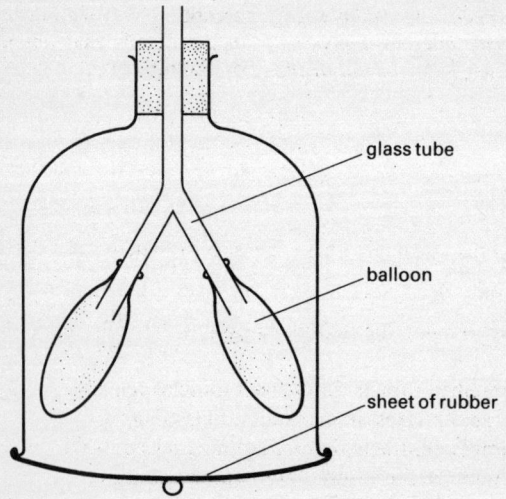

glass tube

balloon

sheet of rubber

Fig. 5.2.

(a) What parts of the body do the balloons represent? (1 mark)

The lungs

Obvious (isn't it?)

(b) What part of the body does the sheet of rubber represent?

(1 mark)

The diaphragm

(c) Explain why the balloons inflate when the rubber sheet is pulled down. (3 marks)

Pulling down the rubber sheet increases the volume (space) inside the bell jar. This creates a negative pressure because the space has to be filled. The walls of the balloons are drawn outwards to fill the space, so air is drawn into them.

Explain this step by step so that you don't get confused.

(d) State *two* ways in which the model does *not* demonstrate inhalation in man. (2 marks)

The lungs are not as simple as balloons. When the diaphragm moves down the intercostal muscles move the rib cage up and out at the same time.

If you know the mechanism of breathing you simply have to fill in the details that are not shown by the model.

Section 2

Work carefully through these questions. There are 35 marks in total.

1. When we inhale, the following things happen (choose the best answer):
    A. diaphragm contracts, intercostal muscles relax
    B. diaphragm relaxes, intercostal muscles relax
    C. diaphragm contracts, intercostal muscles contract
    D. diaphragm relaxes, intercostal muscles contract. (1 mark)

2. Approximately how many alvcoli are there in the human lungs?
    A. 500 million
    B. 100 million
    C. 10 million
    D. 100 000. (1 mark)

3. The maintenance of a flow of water or air over a respiratory surface is called
    A. respiration
    B. gas exchange
    C. breathing
    D. diffusion. (1 mark)

4. Gas exchange in woody plants can take place at the
    A. internodes
    B. girdle scars
    C. axils
    D. lenticels (1 mark)

5. Figure 5.3 represents the gas exchange system of a fish.

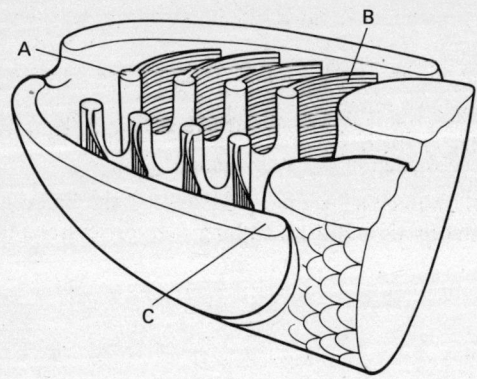

Fig. 5.3.

(a) Name the parts labelled A–C.   (3 marks)
(b) The sentences below describe breathing in fish but they are in the
    wrong order. Starting with water entering the mouth, put the sen-
    tences in the correct order.
    A. The floor of the mouth cavity is lowered and the mouth opens.
       Water enters the mouth.
    B. Water flows out of the body.
    C. The mouth is closed and the floor of the mouth cavity is raised.
    D. The edge of each operculum lifts.
    E. The opercula bulge out, drawing water across the gills.

                                                                    (5 marks)

6. The table shows the rates of oxygen absorption and energy consumption for various activities carried out by humans.

Activity	Oxygen absorption (l/min)	Energy consumption (kJ/min)
Sitting	0·25	5·7
Walking slowly	0·7	12·6
Walking up and down stairs	1·9	38·0
Running	4·2	80·0

(a) What relationship do you notice between oxygen absorption and
    energy consumption? Explain your answer.   (2 marks)

(b) We only **ABSORB** about 25 per cent of the oxygen we breathe in. How much **OXYGEN** must be breathed in for one minute of walking slowly? (2 marks)

(c) **AIR** contains about 20 per cent oxygen. How much **AIR** must be breathed in for two minutes of running? (3 marks)

(d) One gram of bacon provides 20 kJ of energy. How much bacon would we need for ten minutes of running? (2 marks)

7. Figure 5.4 shows the relationship between the amount of carbon dioxide in inhaled air and the breathing rate for several animals.

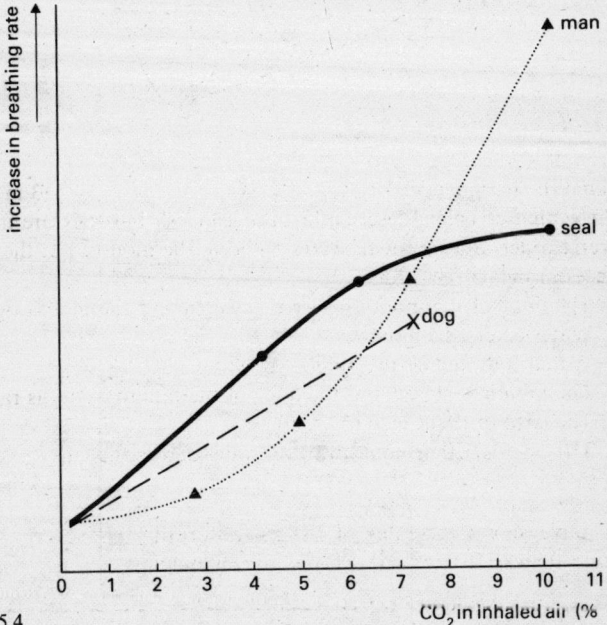

Fig. 5.4

(a) Which animal is least sensitive to carbon dioxide in inhaled air? (1 mark)

(b) Which animal is most sensitive to carbon dioxide in inhaled air? (1 mark)

(c) What does the graph tell you about the control of breathing rate in these animals? (2 marks)

8. Figure 5.5 shows an experiment to investigate the production of carbon dioxide by a mouse.

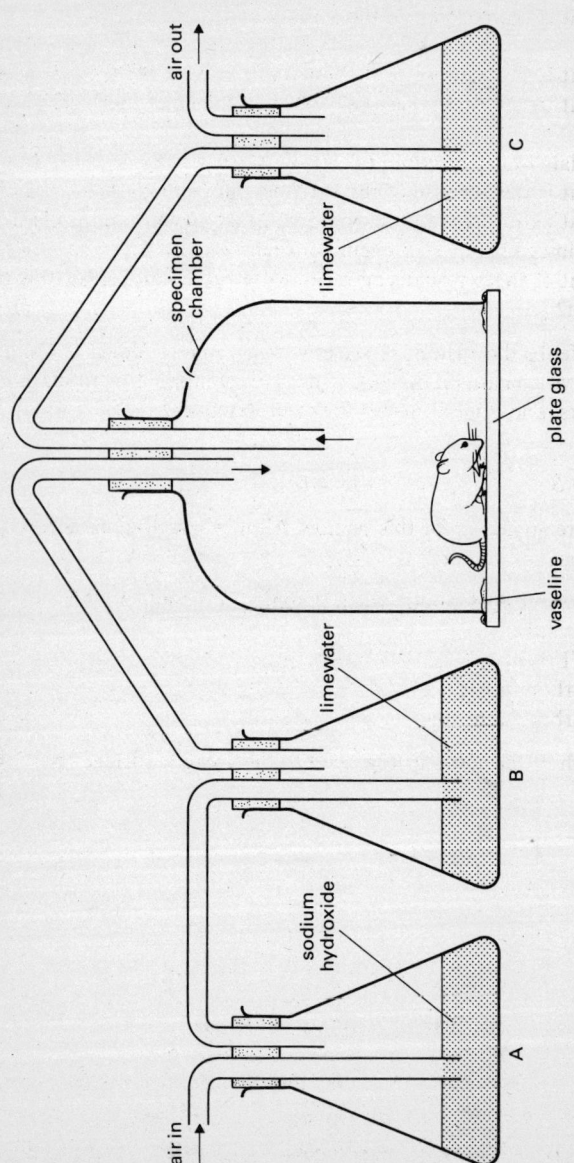

Fig. 5.5.

(a) What is the purpose of the sodium hydroxide in flask A?

(1 mark)

(b) What is the purpose of the limewater in flask B? (1 mark)

(c) What would you expect to happen to the limewater in flask C?

(1 mark)

(d) Explain your answer to (c). (2 marks)

(e) What is the purpose of the vaseline and plate glass? (1 mark)

(f) What extra precautions would you take if you used a plant in the specimen chamber? Explain your answer. (3 marks)

(g) What changes would you make to set up a control for this experiment? (1 mark)

Now refer to the answers to see how well you have done. If you got less than 15 you have a lot of work to do. Give yourself 1 merit mark for 25–30 marks, and 2 merit marks for over 30 marks.

Section 3

There are 40 marks for this section. Allow yourself 45 minutes to show what a genius you are.

1. Limewater goes cloudy when it comes into contact with
   A. oxygen
   B. ATP
   C. carbon dioxide
   D. carbon monoxide. (1 mark)

2. Which of the cubes in Fig. 5.6 has the greatest surface area : volume ratio? (1 mark)

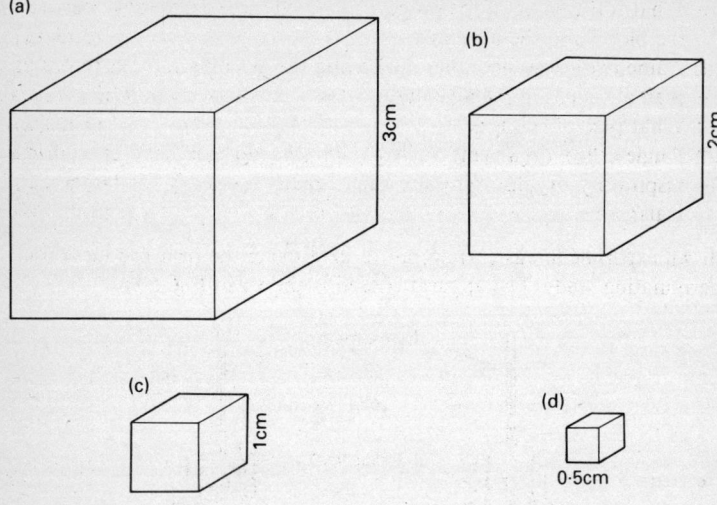

Fig. 5.6.

3. Figure 5.7 shows an alveolus with a capillary in close contact.

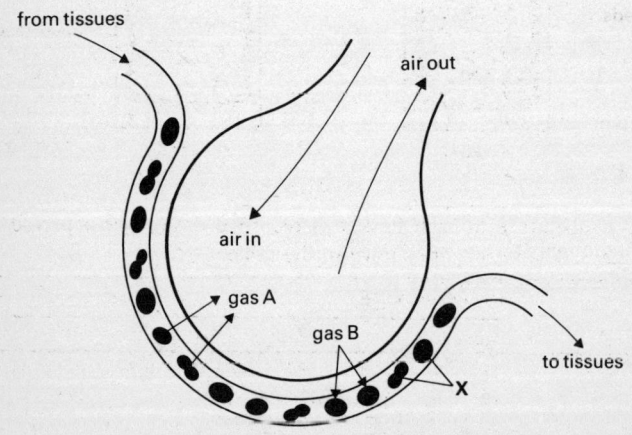

Fig. 5.7.

(a) What is gas A?   (1 mark)
(b) What is gas B?   (1 mark)

(c) What is the name of the process by which these gases move between the blood and the alveolus? (1 mark)
(d) Name two substances that air leaving the alveolus contains more of than air entering the alveolus. (2 marks)
(e) What type of cell is X? (1 mark)
(f) Single-celled organisms such as *Amoeba* do not have specialized respiratory organs. Why are such organs necessary for larger animals? (3 marks)

4. An experiment was carried out to investigate the heat production of germinating seeds. The apparatus used is shown in Fig. 5.8.

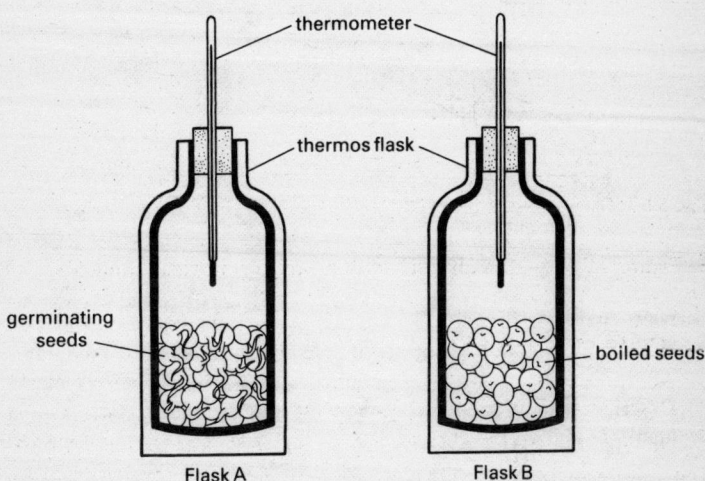

Fig. 5.8.

The temperature in each flask was recorded daily over a period of seven days. The results are shown in the table.

Day	Temperature (°C)	
	Flask A	Flask B
1	18	18
2	19	18
3	20	17
4	21	18
5	22	18
6	24	19
7	25	18

(a) Draw a graph of the results.   (5 marks)
(b) What do you conclude from the results?   (2 marks)

5. Part of the tracheal system of an insect is shown in Fig. 5.9.

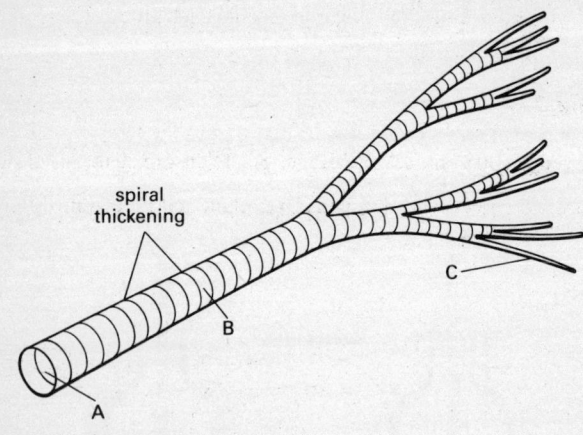

spiral
thickening

C

B

A

Fig. 5.9.

(a) Name parts A, B and C.   (3 marks)
(b) What is the function of the spiral thickenings shown in the diagram?
                                                                                                (1 mark)
(c) Describe two differences between the gas exchange systems of a
    mammal and an insect.   (4 marks)

6. Explain how
(a) a NAMED protozoan,   (2 marks)
(b) an earthworm,   (4 marks)
(c) a frog, and   (4 marks)
(d) a flowering plant   (4 marks)
obtain their supply of oxygen.

Wordsearch

At the risk of spoiling you, a little entertainment is next on the agenda.
You have probably done wordsearches before; this one contains 20
words that have something to do with this chapter. As you find each
word, write it down and beside it write a sentence.

```
S  P  I  R  A  C  L  E  B  U  Z  R  A  S  T  K  X
C  Y  H  A  N  I  H  C  N  O  R  B  N  L  A  O  Z
K  E  M  F  A  B  L  A  N  E  Q  I  P  T  E  E  O
G  J  R  B  E  O  E  M  E  J  T  W  A  R  A  J  S
V  T  N  H  R  R  B  G  M  M  O  M  O  A  A  N  E
P  M  G  B  O  E  D  I  U  P  O  V  L  C  P  O  D
T  U  N  V  B  A  H  D  Y  T  S  G  A  H  G  I  I
P  L  U  H  I  F  T  R  S  B  I  L  L  E  P  T  X
H  L  L  E  C  I  T  N  E  L  V  R  N  O  S  A  O
A  Y  T  R  M  K  C  I  L  E  Q  E  C  L  B  R  I
R  H  W  T  U  F  D  T  O  D  G  C  M  E  I  I  D
Y  P  E  L  B  W  E  L  F  Y  A  R  L  C  E  P  N
N  O  I  T  A  R  I  P  X  E  E  J  S  I  G  S  O
X  S  I  K  G  E  N  O  R  W  D  T  Y  T  D  E  B
B  E  M  H  R  N  P  L  E  U  R  A  L  C  I  R  R
V  M  J  S  A  T  N  D  I  A  P  H  R  A  G  M  A
D  T  F  K  H  F  A  W  Y  F  N  M  C  L  A  W  C
```

Answers

Section 2

1. C   2. A   3. C   4. D   (1 mark each)
5. (a) A. gill bar; B. gill filament; C. operculum   (3 marks)
   (b) A, E, C, D, B   (5 marks)

6.
(a) As oxygen absorption increases, so does energy consumption. This is because oxygen is used in respiration to make energy.   (1 mark)
(b) 0·7 litres of oxygen need to be absorbed to provide the energy for one minute of walking slowly. We need to breathe in four times as much oxygen as we absorb, so we need to breathe in 4 × 0·7 = 2·8 litres.
                                                            (2 marks)

(c) For two minutes of running the oxygen absorbed is $4·2 \times 2 = 8·4$ litres. Oxygen breathed in $= 4 \times 8·4 = 33·6$ litres. Air contains 20 per cent oxygen, so the air breathed in $= 33·6 \times 5 = 168$ litres.

(3 marks)

(d) Ten minutes of running uses $80 \times 10 = 800$ kJ. The amount of bacon required to provide this energy $= 800/20 = 40$ g. (2 marks)

7.
(a) Dog (1 mark)
(b) Man (1 mark)
(c) The graph shows that as more carbon dioxide is exhaled the breathing rate increases. This suggests that the breathing rate is controlled by the amount of carbon dioxide inhaled. (2 marks)

8.
(a) To remove carbon dioxide from air entering the apparatus.

(1 mark)

(b) The limewater shows whether the sodium hydroxide has removed all of the carbon dioxide entering the apparatus. (1 mark)
(c) The limewater in C would go cloudy. (1 mark)
(d) The limewater in C would go cloudy because it receives the exhaled air, which contains carbon dioxide, from the mouse. (2 marks)
(e) The vaseline and plate glass provide a seal to prevent air from entering the bell jar at the bottom. (1 mark)
(f) For a plant the bell jar should be covered to prevent light entering. If the plant received light it would photosynthesize using the carbon dioxide produced in respiration. (3 marks)
(g) In a control experiment there should be no organism in the bell jar.

(1 mark)

Section 3

1. B   2. D (1 mark each)
3.
(a) Oxygen. (1 mark)
(b) Carbon dioxide. (1 mark)
(c) Diffusion. (1 mark)
(d) Carbon dioxide and water vapour. (2 marks)
(e) Red blood cell. (1 mark)
(f) In *Amoeba*, oxygen can diffuse in from the water and carbon dioxide can diffuse out. As *Amoeba* is very small it has a large surface area : volume ratio, so that enough gas exchange can take place across the

surface to deal with the *Amoeba's* requirements. In larger animals, most of the body is too far away from the surface for the gases to diffuse quickly enough between them. These animals need a method of transporting gases to and from the outside to overcome these problems. (3 marks)

4.
(a)

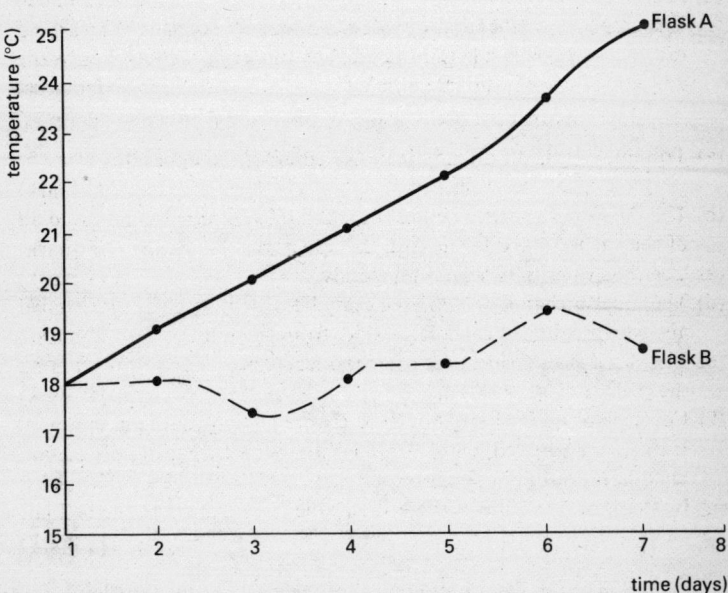

Fig. 5.10.

(b) The results show that germinating seeds produce heat whereas dead seeds do not. This heat probably comes from respiration, but the experiment does not show this. (2 marks)

5.
(a) A. spiracle; B. trachea; C. tracheole (3 marks)
(b) They stop the trachea collapsing. (1 mark)
(c) Note: when comparing things it is often best to put it in table form:

Insect	Mammal
Gas exchange system is spread throughout the body	Gas exchange system is localized (in one place; i.e. the lungs)
Oxygen and carbon dioxide are carried to and from the cells in air.	Oxygen and carbon dioxide are exchanged between the air in the alveoli and the blood. The air does not come into direct contact with the cells

(4 marks)

6.

(a) Remember to NAME the protozoan; e.g. *Amoeba*. In *Amoeba* oxygen diffuses from the surrounding water into the cell.

(2 marks)

(b) Earthworms use their body surface to obtain oxygen. The epidermis of the skin is covered in mucus. Oxygen dissolves in the mucus and then diffuses into capillaries just below the epidermis.

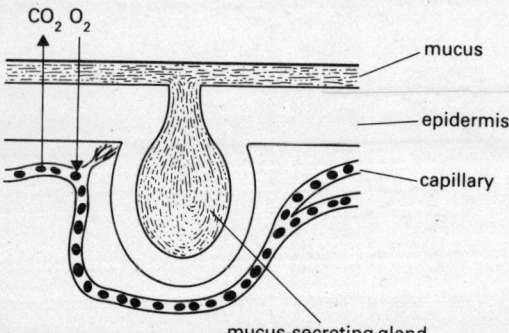

Fig. 5.11.   (4 marks)

(c) When in water, frogs obtain most of their oxygen by diffusion across the surface of the skin. The skin has a rich supply of capillaries to take up the oxygen. On land, oxygen is taken up across the mouth lining when the frog is inactive. When active, the lungs are used.

(4 marks)

(d) Plants exchange gases with the atmosphere through the stomatal pores. Oxygen entering the plant through these pores is taken up across the surfaces of the spongy mesophyll cells.

   During the day, oxygen is produced by photosynthesis, and usually the plant does not need more oxygen from the atmosphere. At night the plant continues to respire but photosynthesis stops, so the plant takes up oxygen from outside.

Woody plants, such as trees, also have lenticels for gas exchange. These are small pores in the bark through which oxygen can be taken up and then diffuse into cells below the bark.　　　　(4 marks)

Wordsearch: words to be found

Spiracle, aerobic, bronchi, haemoglobin, gill, stomata, tracheole, lenticel, lung, pleural, expiration, pharynx, oxygen, mesophyll, carbon dioxide, anaerobic, diaphragm, alveoli, lactic, respiration.

6. Transport

There is a continual exchange of substances between organisms and their environment. For small organisms this is no problem because of their large surface area:volume ratio. Larger organisms require specialized parts to deal with this exchange. As a result, they need to have a transport system to move substances to and from these areas. A transport system is also useful for moving things from one part of an organism to another.

In this chapter we are concerned with the transport systems of mammals and flowering plants.

Section 1

1.

Look carefully at Fig. 6.1 and answer the questions.

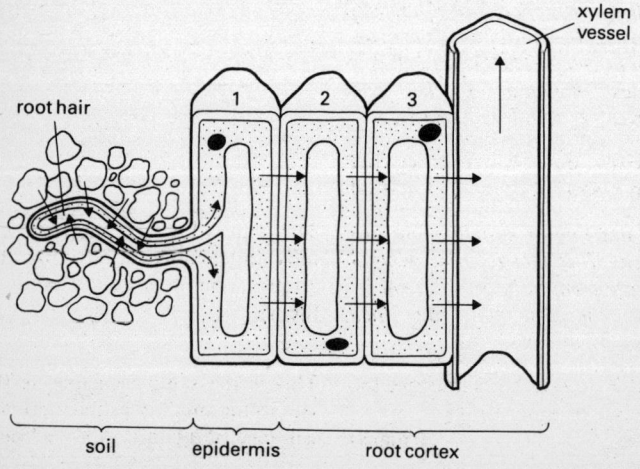

Fig. 6.1.

QUESTION

COMMENT

(a) Explain why water should enter the root hair from the soil.
(2 marks)

The cytoplasm in the root hair is a stronger solution than the water in the soil. Therefore water enters the root hair by osmosis, the cell membrane acting as a selectively permeable membrane.

Always remember that cytoplasm contains many dissolved substances so that it has a higher osmotic pressure (OP) than water. Call it semi-permeable if you like, but 'selectively' is better.

(b) What effect does water entering cell 1 have on its OP? (1 mark)

Water entering cell 1 dilutes the cytoplasm so that the OP decreases.

Any dilution of cytoplasm must have this effect.

(c) Explain the steps that lead to water passing into cell 3.
(3 marks)

You already have the information you need if you answered (b). Take it step-by-step and you won't get confused (hopefully).

As the cytoplasm of cell 1 is diluted, its OP is now less than that of cell 2; water therefore enters cell 2 by osmosis, thus diluting the cytoplasm of cell 2. The OP of cell 2 is now less than that of cell 3 and water enters cell 3 by osmosis.

(d) How does water enter the xylem vessel? (3 marks)

It is not known exactly how this happens. It is thought that mineral salts are pumped into the xylem by active transport and water then follows by osmosis.

There are a lot of things we don't fully understand but have theories about. You must say that it is theory.

(e) How do root hairs improve the efficiency of water uptake?
(1 mark)

This is the same principle as the villi in the small intestine, and you will meet it again in other areas.

The root hairs increase the surface area for uptake of water.

2.

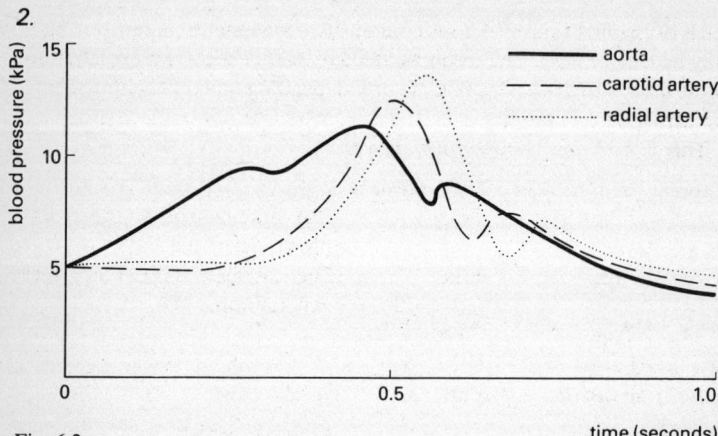

Fig. 6.2.

When you take your pulse you usually feel the radial artery at your wrist. Pulses can be taken at other places in the body. Figure 6.2 is a graph showing the pulses in three blood vessels.

(a) In which of these three vessels does the pulse occur first?
(1 mark)

From the graph you can see that the pressure in the aorta begins to rise first.

Aorta.

(b) In which vessel does the pulse occur last?   (1 mark)

Again, read this from the graph.

Radial artery.

(c) Explain why the pulse occurs at different times in different vessels.

Each pulse begins at the heart. The pressure from the heart reaches the aorta first because it is nearer the heart. The next nearest vessel is the carotid artery and of the three vessels the radial artery is the furthest away. Therefore the wave of pressure from the heart reaches the radial artery last.

Let's hope you get (a) and (b) right or your explanation here will probably be wrong. You need to know where the arteries are to answer this bit, but otherwise it's quite straightforward.

Section 2

Each of the first four questions contains two statements, either of which may be true or false. The second statement *may* be a correct explanation of the first. You answer A, B, C, D or E depending on how the statements are arranged.

This is how you choose your answer:

Answer	1st statement	2nd statement	
A	True	True	2nd statement is a correct explanation of the 1st
B	True	True	2nd statement is NOT a correct explanation.
C	True	False	
D	False	True	
E	False	False	

1ST STATEMENT	2ND STATEMENT
1. The wall of the left ventricle is thicker than that of the right ventricle.	The left ventricle receives more blood than the right. (1 mark)
2. Transpiration is faster on a hot, dry day than on a hot humid day.	Water evaporates into hot dry air faster than into hot humid air. (1 mark)
3. If cobalt chloride paper were clamped to the upper and lower surfaces of a leaf, the paper on the upper surface would turn pink first.	Cobalt chloride turns pink when exposed to carbon dioxide. (1 mark)
4. The pulmonary artery carries blood from the lungs to the heart.	The pulmonary artery contains less oxygen than the pulmonary vein. (1 mark)

5. Figure 6.3 shows a section through a human heart.
(a) Name the structures labelled A–E. (5 marks)
(b) Explain why the wall of the left ventricle is thicker than the wall of the right ventricle. (2 marks)
(c) If part C was not working properly the blood cells would not flow efficiently. Why do you think this is? (3 marks)
(d) The sentences below describe the different stages of one heart beat but they are in the wrong order. Starting with blood entering the right atrium, show the correct sequence of events. (6 marks)

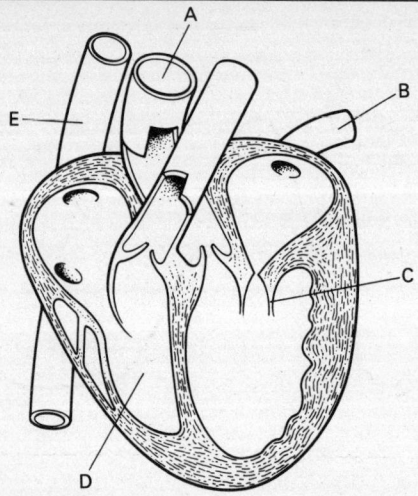

Fig. 6.3.

A. The left atrium contracts and blood is pushed into the left ventricle. Valves in the pulmonary vein prevent blood from re-entering the atrium.

B. The right ventricle contracts. The tricuspid valve stops blood going back into the right atrium, so blood is pushed into the pulmonary artery.

C. At the lungs the blood loses carbon dioxide and collects oxygen; it then enters the pulmonary vein.

D. Blood enters the right atrium from the vena cava.

E. The left ventricle contracts. The bicuspid valve will not allow the blood to go back into the left atrium, so the pressure forces the blood into the aorta.

F. The right atrium contracts. Blood is prevented from going back into the vena cava by a valve, so blood is pushed into the right ventricle.

G. Blood in the aorta travels to the head and body. The semi-lunar valve stops blood going back into the left ventricle.

H. Blood from the pulmonary vein enters the left atrium.

I. The blood travels along the pulmonary artery to the lungs. The semi-lunar valve stops blood moving back into the right ventricle.

(6 marks)

(e) Figure 6.4 shows the changes in the volume and pressure of blood in the left ventricle of a mammal during one heart beat.

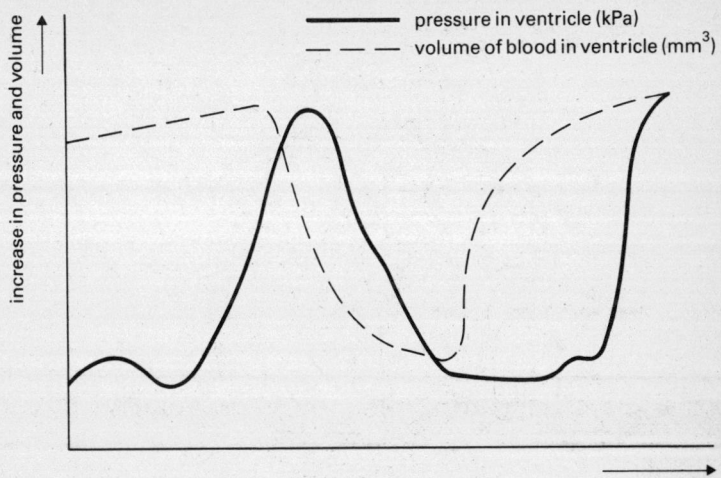

Fig. 6.4.

    (i) What relationship do you notice between the volume of blood in the ventricle and the blood pressure? (2 marks)

    (ii) Explain why this relationship occurs. (3 marks)

(f) Why is the blood pressure in the arteries greater than that in the veins? (2 marks)

(g) With the aid of labelled diagrams, describe how blood is moved along the veins. (5 marks)

(h) Sometimes, when guardsmen stand to attention for a long time, they faint. This is because their blood does not circulate properly. Why do you think this is? (2 marks)

6. Figure 6.5 shows the movement of water through a leaf.

(a) Describe what happens to water from the time it reaches the leaf in the xylem vessel to the time it leaves the leaf. Be sure to explain *why* the water moves through the leaf. (5 marks)

(b) How would you measure the rate of transpiration in a flowering plant? Use diagrams to show the apparatus you would use.

(5 marks)

(c) Name three environmental factors that affect the rate of transpiration. Explain what effect each has and why. (6 marks)

(d) Read the passage on p. 76 and choose the best word for each of (i) to (v).

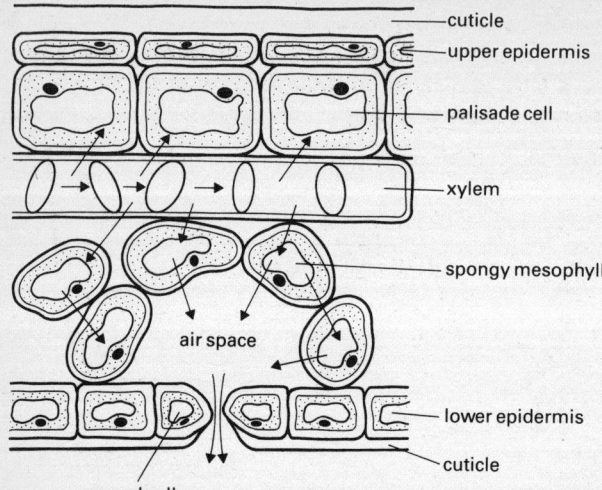

Fig. 6.5.

Plants take up water at the roots through the root hairs. The water passes through the cells of the root [(i) vortex, cortex, matrix] to the xylem [(ii) vessels, tubes, elements]. It is pushed some of the way up the xylem by root pressure, but this is not powerful enough for the water to reach the top of the plant. Transport of water to the uppermost parts is achieved by the process of [(iii) transpiration, transduction, translocation] which involves the [(iv) condensation, osmosis, evaporation] of water through the [(v) mesophyll, cuticle, stomata].   (5 marks)

7. Figure 6.6 shows a transverse section of the stem of a herbaceous dicotyledon.

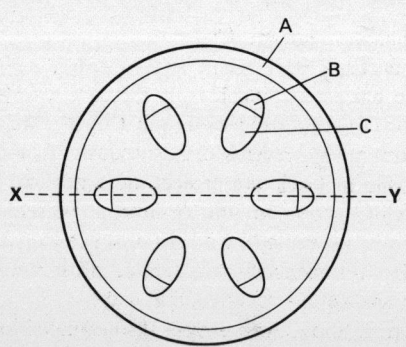

Fig. 6.6.

(a) Name the parts labelled A–C. (3 marks)
(b) What is the name of parts B and C combined? (1 mark)
(c) Draw a labelled diagram to show the view of the stem if cut longitudinally along line X–Y. (4 marks)

8. The flow chart shows the sequence of events in blood clot formation.

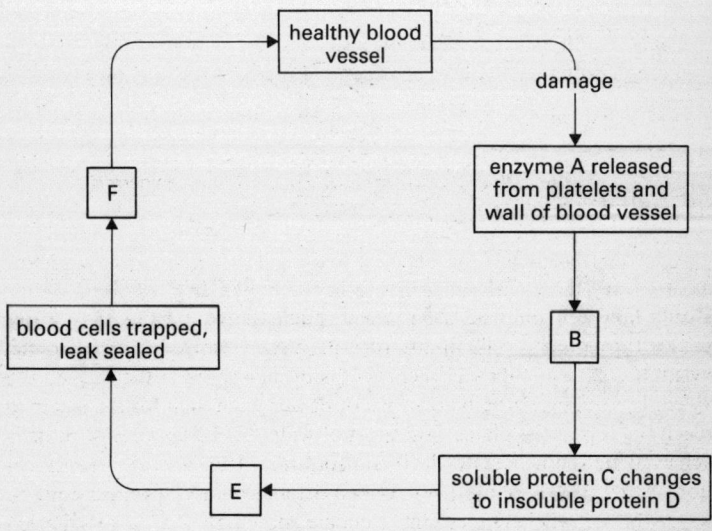

(a) What is the name of enzyme A? (1 mark)
(b) What events occur at B? (2 marks)
(c) Name the two proteins C and D. (2 marks)
(d) Describe the events that occur at E and F. (4 marks)
(e) Blood clot formation prevents excessive loss of blood.. Name one other way in which it helps to protect the organism. (1 mark)
(f) For a blood clot to form, vitamin K must be present. The action of vitamin K can be prevented by a rat poison called warfarin. People who suffer from thrombosis are treated with small amounts of warfarin. Explain. (3 marks)
(g) The table on p. 78 shows who people of four main blood groups can donate blood to or receive blood from.

Blood group	Donate to	Receive from
A	A, AB	(i)
B	B, (ii)	O, B
AB	(iii)	O, A, B, AB
O	(iv)	O

What blood group or groups do (i) to (iv) represent?   (4 marks)

There are 80 marks for Section 2 (quite a lot eh?) If you get over 50 you're not doing badly. Over 65 is good (1 merit); over 70 is very good (2 merits).

Section 3

You haven't been cheating on these Section 3 questions have you? Remember, try them without referring to the books, it gives you a better idea of how well your revision is going. There is quite a lot to do so allow yourself an hour.

1. Blood plasma contains how much water?
   A. 75%
   B. 92%
   C. 99%
   D. 60%   (1 mark)

2. Which vessel contains the highest oxygen concentration?
   A. vena cava
   B. renal vein
   C. pulmonary vein
   D. hepatic vein.   (1 mark)

Questions 3 to 5 refer to some of the following tissues in a green plant:
   A. phloem
   B. xylem
   C. spongy mesophyll
   D. cortex
   E. cambium.
Each of the descriptions in questions 3 to 5 refers to one of the tissues above. State which is which.

3. Transports water and mineral salts through the plant.   (1 mark)

4. Made up of living cells which are connected at their ends by sieve plates. (1 mark)

5. Region of cell division. (1 mark)

6.

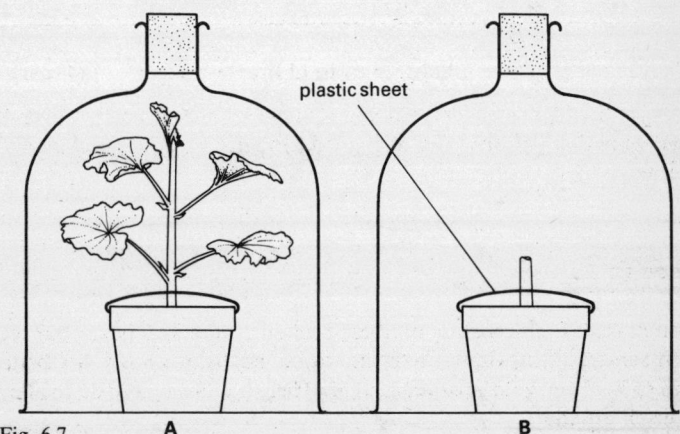

Fig. 6.7.   **A**   **B**

Bell jar A contains a leafy geranium, B contains a geranium with the leaves and upper parts of the stem removed.

(a) If both jars were left in sunlight for 12 hours, what would you expect to happen? Explain your answer. (4 marks)

(b) With the aid of labelled diagrams, explain how the turgidity of the guard cells controls the opening and closing of the stomata. (6 marks)

(c) Figure 6.8 shows a cross-section of the leaf of marram grass. In dry conditions the leaf folds inwards. How does this help conserve water? (3 marks)

7. Figure 6.9 shows some of the constituents of blood as seen under a microscope.

(a) Name two functions for the cell labelled A. (2 marks)

(b) In which part of the blood would glucose and amino acids be carried? (1 mark)

(c) Use labelled diagrams to show how cell B would destroy a bacterium that entered the blood stream. (4 marks)

(d) Red blood cells live for about 100 days only. Give one reason for their life being so short. (1 mark)

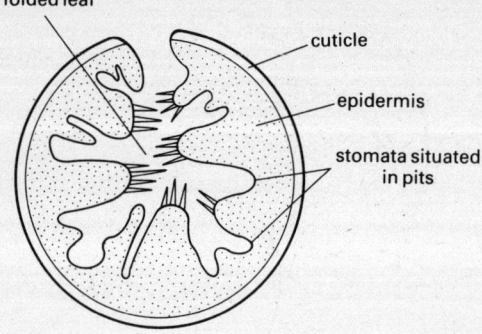

Fig. 6.8.

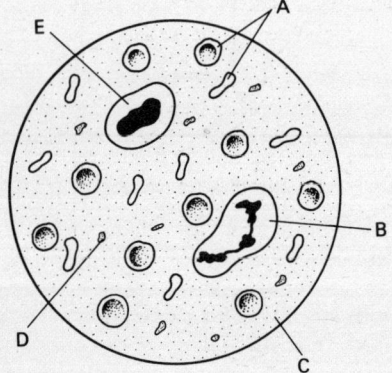

Fig. 6.9.

(e) The average person has about 5 litres of blood. In each cubic millimetre of blood there are about 400 000 platelets. How many platelets are there in the average person?   (2 marks)

8. Figure 6.10 shows the circulatory system of a human.
(a) Name the parts labelled A–F.   (6 marks)
(b) Which blood vessel has to withstand most pressure?   (1 mark)
(c) Name one difference between the blood in vessel B and the blood in vessel C.   (1 mark)

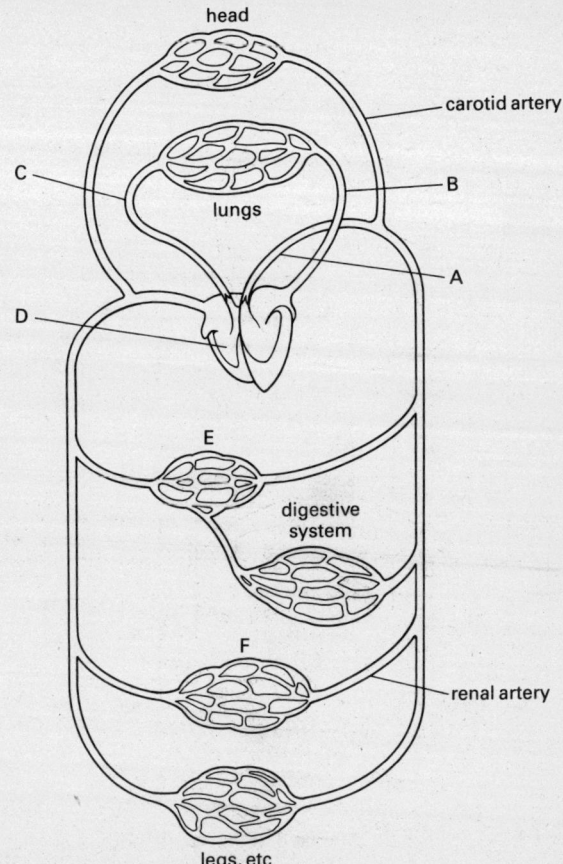

Fig. 6.10.

(d) Aspirin is absorbed into the bloodstream through the walls of the
    stomach. Describe the route taken by a molecule of aspirin from the
    time it leaves the stomach to the time it eases a headache.

    (9 marks)

There are 45 marks for Section 3. Check your answers. Over 30 is
good, over 40 is excellent.

Crossword

Yes, that's right, another crossword, but a bit harder than the last one. You can check you answers with those at the end of this chapter.

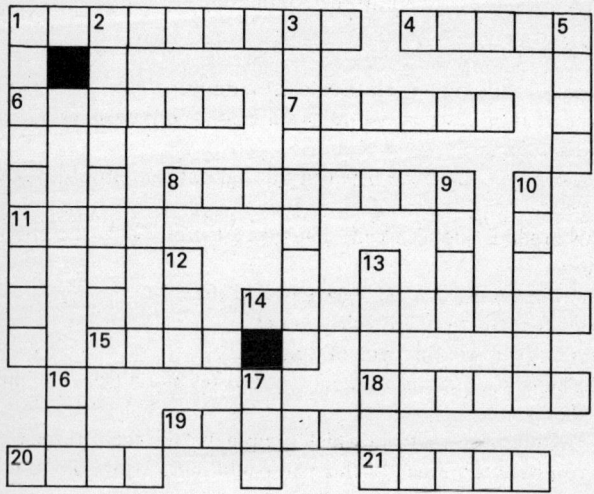

Fig. 6.11.

Clues

Across

1. When a blood vessel is damaged these small bodies in the blood produce chemicals which help to convert fibrinogen to fibrin.
4. This word is used to refer to the kidney and is also the name of an artery and a vein associated with the kidney.
6. General name for the type of blood vessel that carries blood, usually oxygenated, but not always, away from the heart.
7. Phagocytic white blood cells do this to bacteria.
8. The name of the valve between the left atrium and the left ventricle.
11. This is formed when a network of fibrin fibres builds up across a wound.
14. Red blood cells are usually described as being this shape.
15. A site on a lymph vessel where antibodies and new white blood cells are formed.

18. Type of fly that spreads sleeping sickness by sucking blood.
19. The liquid part of blood which is mainly water but contains many dissolved substances (e.g. glucose, amino acids, urea).
20. This metal is found in the haemoglobin molecule.
21. This is formed when excess tissue fluid, which does not re-enter the capillaries, is drained into the lymphatics.

Down

1. Type of white blood cell that 'eats' pathogens.
2. Type of antibody that neutralizes the poisonous chemicals produced by bacteria.
3. The name of the valve between the right atrium and the right ventricle.
5. This organ is supplied with de-oxygenated blood by the pulmonary artery.
9. A red blood cell is a biconcave one of these.
10. Veins have these but arteries do not.
12. Erythrocytes are this type of blood cell.
13. The hepatic .... vein takes blood from the intestines to the liver.
16. A mixture of gases from which mammals take their oxygen.
17. If you have too much of this you could put a strain on your heart.

Answers

Section 2

1. C   2. A   3. E   4. D   (1 mark each)
5.
(a) A. aorta, B. pulmonary vein; C. bicuspid valve; D. right ventricle; E. vena cava.   (5 marks)
(b) The left ventricle pushes blood around the body whereas the right ventricle has to push blood only as far as the lungs. The left ventricle, therefore, requires a thicker muscular wall to force the blood over a greater distance than the right ventricle.   (2 marks)
(c) Part C is the bicuspid valve which prevents back-flow of blood into the left atrium when the left ventricle contracts. If the valve were not working properly some of the blood from the left ventricle would be forced into the left atrium instead of going to the rest of the body.   (3 marks)

(d) The sentences should be in this order:
 D, F, B, I, C, H, A, E, G.   (6 marks)
(e) (i) The pressure in the ventricle rises and, shortly before it reaches a maximum, the volume starts to fall. The volume of blood then rises to a maximum before the pressure starts to build up again.
                                                              (2 marks)
  (ii) The volume of blood in the ventricle increases until it is full. When full, the muscular walls of the ventricle start to contract, increasing the pressure of the blood. This pressure forces blood into the aorta so the volume of blood in the ventricle decreases. As the wall of the ventricle relaxes the pressure decreases and blood enters the ventricle again, increasing the volume.
                                                              (3 marks)
(f) The arteries receive blood, under pressure, from the heart. The veins receive blood from the capillaries in the tissues. By the time the blood passes into the veins the pressure has been reduced considerably during its passage through the capillaries.   (2 marks)
(g) Contraction of muscles squeezes the veins, pushing blood along them.

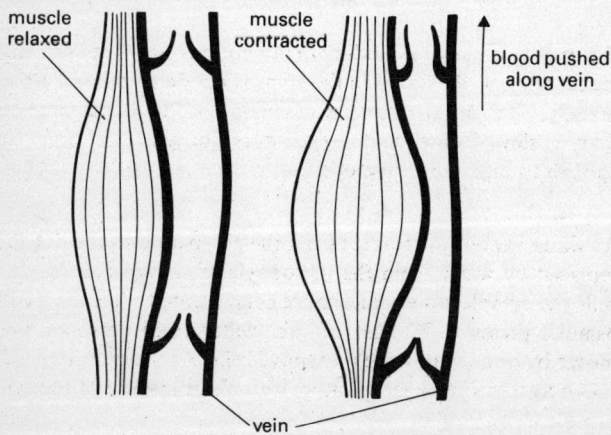

Fig. 6.12.

Valves in the veins ensure that blood only flows in one direction; i.e. towards the heart.

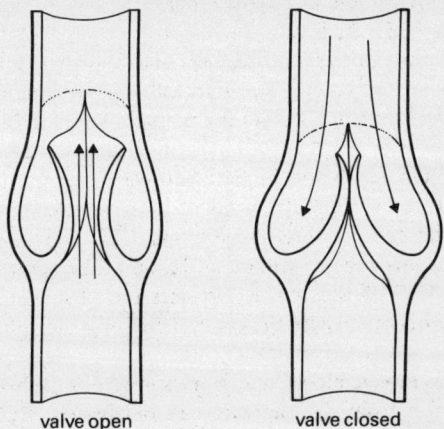

valve open   valve closed

Fig. 6.13.

Also, the walls of the veins are thinner than those of the arteries, so the blood is able to move along inside the veins more easily.

(5 marks)

(h) When guardsmen are standing to attention they are not moving their leg muscles, so the blood in the veins is not being pushed along very quickly. This means that the circulation of blood throughout the body is slowed down and oxygen does not reach the brain quickly enough to maintain consciousness. (2 marks)

6.

(a) As water vapour evaporates from the air space into the outside, it is replaced by water from the mesophyll cells. As water leaves these cells the cytoplasm becomes more concentrated, thus increasing the osmotic pressure. Because of this, water from neighbouring cells moves by osmosis into the mesophyll cells. As the cytoplasm of these cells becomes a stronger solution, water is drawn out of the xylem by osmosis. (5 marks)

(b) The rate of transpiration can be measured using a potometer.

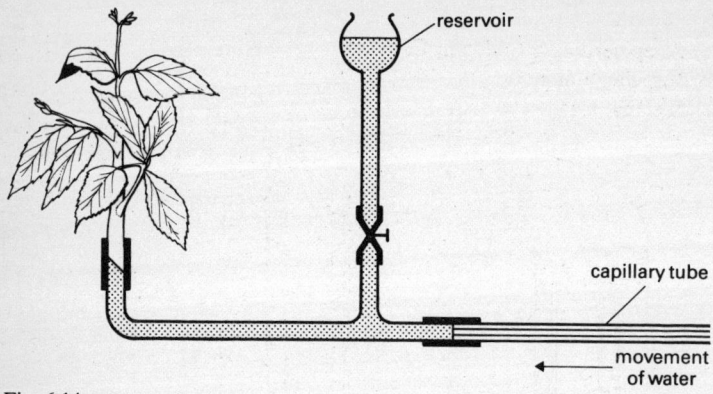

Fig. 6.14.

The shoot draws water through the capillary tube by transpiration. If an air bubble is introduced into the capillary tube, the speed at which it travels over a certain distance gives a measure of the rate of transpiration. Releasing water from the reservoir into the capillary tube pushes the air bubble back to the end of the capillary tube.

(5 marks)

(c) Three of these:

Temperature. Warm air can hold more water vapour than cool air, so on a warm day the evaporation of water from leaves is greater and the transpiration rate is faster.

Windspeed. Air can only hold a certain amount of water vapour. If the air is still, the atmosphere around a leaf can quickly become saturated with water vapour. On a windy day the air around the leaf is being continuously replaced and water continues to evaporate.

Humidity. Humidity is the amount of water vapour in the air. The higher it is the less capacity the air has for more water to evaporate into it. Therefore the transpiration rate is less on a humid day.

Sunshine. When guard cells photosynthesize they make sugars which increase the osmotic pressure of the cytoplasm. They then take up more water from neighbouring cells, becoming turgid. The turgor pressure on the walls of the guard cells causes the stoma to open, increasing the rate of evaporation when other conditions permit.

(6 marks)

(d) (i) cortex; (ii) vessels; (iii) transpiration; (iv) evaporation; (v) stomata.

(5 marks)

7.
(a) A. epidermis; B. phloem; C. xylem. (3 marks)
(b) vascular bundle (1 mark)
(c) See Fig. 6.15.

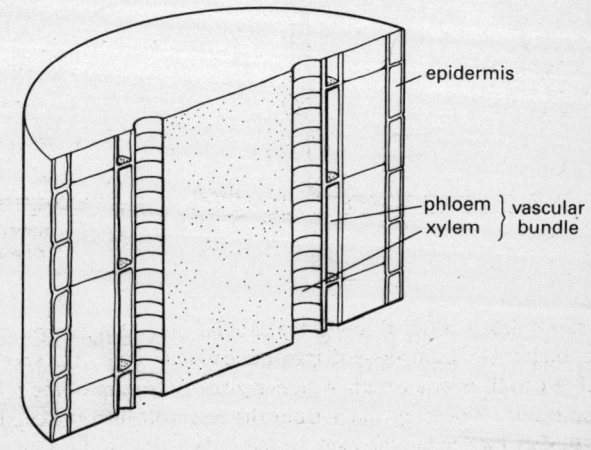

Fig. 6.15. (4 marks)

8.
(a) Thrombokinase. (1 mark)
(b) Prothrombin is activated to thrombin (2 marks)
(c) C. Fibrinogen; D. Fibrin. (2 marks)
(d) E. A mesh of fibres is formed at the site of the wound; F. A scab forms and the wound heals. (4 marks)
(e) It also prevents the entry of infectious organisms. (1 mark)
(f) Thrombosis is caused by blood clots forming in the blood vessels, blocking them. Warfarin prevents blood clotting, thus easing the thrombosis. (3 marks)
(g) (i) O, A; (ii) AB; (iii) AB; (iv) O, A, B, AB. (4 marks)

Section 3

1. B   2. C   3. B   4. A   5. E   (1 mark each)
6.
(a) Condensation would form on the inside of bell jar A because water has evaporated from the plant through the stomata in the leaves. The plant in bell jar B has no leaves; therefore there is no evaporation of water from the plant and no condensation forms. (4 marks)

(b)

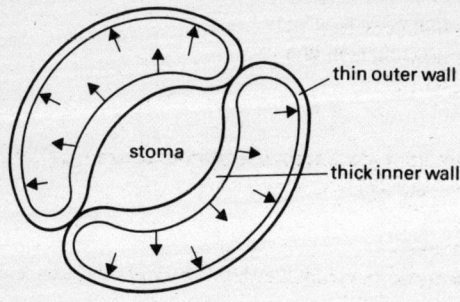

Fig. 6.16.

The inner walls of the guard cells are thicker than the outer walls. When the guard cell is turgid the thinner outer wall is pushed outward. The inner wall is drawn into the cell as a result, opening the stoma. (6 marks)

(c) When the leaf is turned in, the stomata all face into a small area. Water vapour from the leaf enters this space and saturates the air. As this cannot move away from the leaf quickly the rate of transpiration slows down so that less water is lost from the plant (3 marks)

7.

(a) Transport of oxygen and carbon dioxide. (2 marks)
(b) C. Plasma. (1 mark)
(c)

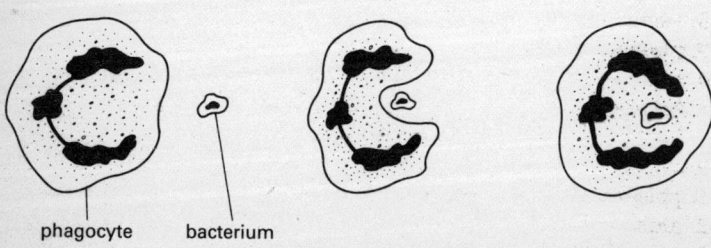

phagocyte   bacterium

Fig. 6.17. (4 marks)

(d) Red blood cells have no nucleus. (1 mark)

(e) 400 000 per mm^3
    400 000 × 1000 per litre
    = 400 000 000 per litre.
    In 5 litres, 400 000 000 × 5
    = 2 000 000 000.

8.
(a) A. aorta; B. pulmonary vein; C. pulmonary artery; D. right ventricle;
    E. liver; F. kidneys.   (6 marks)
(b) The aorta.   (1 mark)
(c) Either of these:
    B contains more oxygen than C *or* B contains less carbon dioxide
    than C.   (1 mark)
(d) The places visited by the aspirin molecule are in this order:
    Stomach, hepatic portal vein, liver, hepatic vein, vena cava, right
    atrium, right ventricle, pulmonary artery, lungs, pulmonary vein, left
    atrium, left ventricle, aorta, carotid artery, head.   (9 marks)

Answers to Crossword

Across
 1. platelets
 4. renal
 6. artery
 7. ingest
 8. bicuspid
11. clot
14. biconcave
15. node
18. tsetse
19. plasma
20. iron
21. lymph

Down
 1. phagocyte
 2. antitoxin
 3. tricuspid
 5. lung
 9. disc
10. valves

12. red
13. portal
16. air
17. fat

7. Keeping Conditions in the Body Constant (Homeostasis)

Homeostasis keeps the processes of the body working efficiently by maintaining the internal conditions at an optimum. Although homeostasis involves many different mechanisms we will concentrate on the main ones; that is, excretion, osmoregulation and body temperature in mammals.

Section 1

The Section 1 questions in previous chapters have been split into several parts (a, b, c, etc), a style used by all of the examination boards. The question in this section is of the essay type, where *you* have to decide what information to include and in what order to use it.

Obviously, 'knowing your stuff' is the most important part of writing an essay. Planning is also extremely important. If you try to write an essay without planning you will lose the thread of what you are trying to say, you will lose the examiner's interest and you will lose marks. If you have 30 minutes for an essay you can afford to spend five minutes planning. Write down, in pencil, what you think you should mention and what order it should be in, then draw a line through it to show that it is not part of your essay.

QUESTION

1. Describe
(a) the role of the skin in controlling body temperature.
                    (10 marks)
(b) the role of the kidney in osmoregulation.   (10 marks)

Mention these points:
(a) *The skin surrounds the body, so its role in temperature regulation is to control the movement of heat out*

COMMENT

Note – 10 marks for each part, so spend equal time on each.

I do not intend to write the essay for you, but I will show you what should be included.

of the body. The body needs to lose more heat when it is hot than when it is cold; this is achieved in the following ways:

(i) *Contraction of erector muscles raises hairs, trapping air. Layers of air provide insulation, reducing heat loss. On a hot day, the hairs are lowered.*

(ii) *Many mammals that live in cold areas have a layer of fat (blubber) to prevent heat loss.*

(iii) *On a hot day, capillaries near the surface dilate (get wider) and carry more blood to the surface, allowing more heat to be lost from the blood. On a cold day the opposite happens and blood flow to the skin is reduced.*

Always use some sort of introductory paragraph.

It is perfectly acceptable to split the question into parts, (i), (ii), etc, if you find it easier AND if it makes the answer clearer. Some questions cannot be divided like this.

It is a good idea to use a diagram to illustrate this sort of thing.

HOT DAY

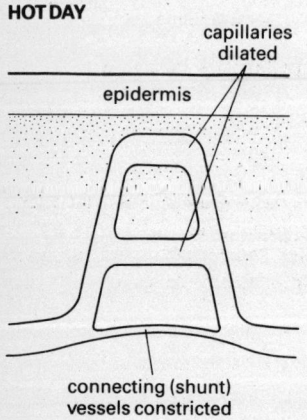

capillaries dilated

epidermis

connecting (shunt) vessels constricted

COLD DAY

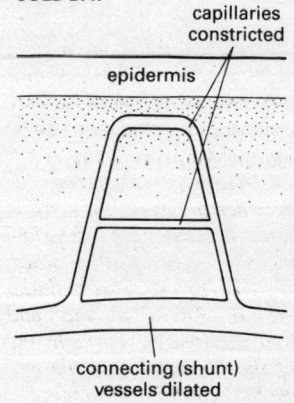

capillaries constricted

epidermis

connecting (shunt) vessels dilated

Fig. 7.1.

(iv) *Evaporation of sweat from the surface of the skin carries heat away from the blood below. So on a hot day more sweat is produced by the sweat glands and this increases the rate of cooling.*

(10 marks)

(b)

If you're going to talk about a structure it is a good idea to use a diagram to show what parts it has, especially if you're going to refer to them.

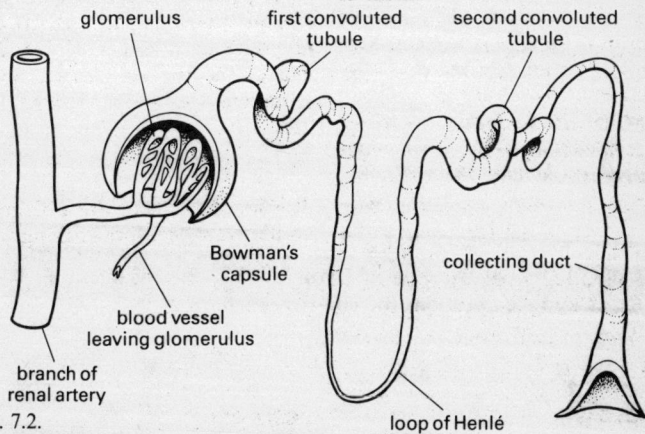

glomerulus | first convoluted tubule | second convoluted tubule

Bowman's capsule

collecting duct

blood vessel leaving glomerulus

branch of renal artery

Fig. 7.2.

loop of Henlé

Each kidney has about one million nephrons, one of which is shown above. The way in which the kidney is involved in osmoregulation can be divided into two parts.

Introductory bit again.

(i) Ultrafiltration – this means filtration under pressure. Pressure is produced because the arteriole entering the glomerulus is wider than the one leaving. This build-up of pressure forces plasma and dissolved substances through the wall of the Bowman's capsule and into the first convoluted tubule.

Having drawn and labelled a nephron (Fig. 7.2.) you can just refer to the parts without further explanation – saves a lot of words.

(ii) Selective reabsorption – much of the content of the glomerular filtrate is needed by the body. These substances are taken back into the blood (reabsorbed). Salts are reabsorbed, by active transport, in both sections of the convoluted tubule.

Water is reabsorbed by osmosis,

Your main concern is with salts and water because the question is about osmoregulation. So leave out excretion – you shouldn't have time to mention it anyway.

mainly in the first convoluted tubule but also in the rest of the tubule. The amount of reabsorption of water in the second convoluted tubule and the collecting duct is controlled by a hormone, anti-diuretic hormone (A D H). When the body needs to reabsorb more water, A D H is released from the pituitary gland. At the nephron it increases the permeability of the second convoluted tubule and the collecting duct so more water is reabsorbed.

As you will have seen (hopefully) it is important to know what to leave out of an essay, which is why you M U S T read the question. There will be essay-type questions for you to try later on.

Section 2

1. Urine is carried from the pelvis of the kidneys to the bladder by the
   A. ureter
   B. urethra
   C. nephron
   D. renal vein.   (1 mark)

2. Most urea is absorbed into the blood as it passes through the
   A. kidney
   B. liver
   C. lungs
   D. pancreas.   (1 mark)

3. The fluid which enters the kidney tubule from the glomerulus does so by a process of
   A. diffusion
   B. osmosis
   C. active transport
   D. ultrafiltration.   (1 mark)

4. Which of the following best describes the events that occur when the body is too hot?
   A. Blood vessels in skin constrict, sweat produced.
   B. Blood vessels in skin dilate, hairs erect.

   C. Blood vessels in skin constrict, hairs erect.

   D. Blood vessels in skin dilate, sweat produced.   (1 mark)

5. Two excretory products of a mammal are

   A. oxygen and urea

   B. carbon dioxide and glucose

   C. carbon dioxide and urea

   D. nitrogen and urea.   (1 mark)

6.

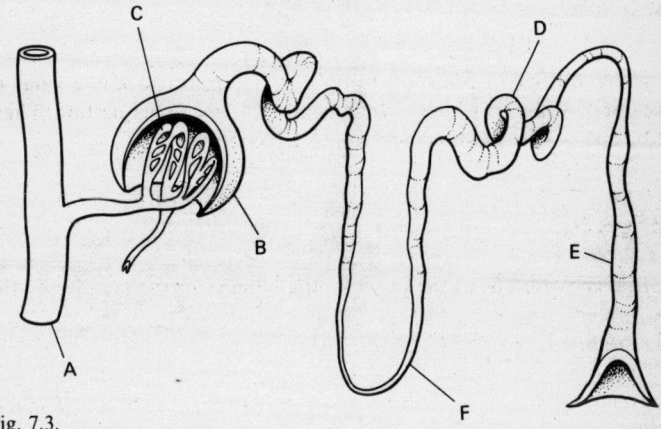

Fig. 7.3.

(a) Name the parts labelled A–F.   (6 marks)

(b) Name the process that occurs at C and explain why it happens.

     (2 marks)

(c) What happens along the length of D?   (2 marks)

(d) Why is F relatively longer in some desert mammals?   (2 marks)

(e) Name two substances that you would expect to find in E.

     (2 marks)

(f) Use ticks or crosses to indicate which substances are present or absent in the fluids shown in the table.

Substance	Blood in A	Liquid in B	Liquid in E
Glucose			
Urea			
Protein			

     (9 marks)

(g) Draw a labelled diagram of a section through a kidney to show where *one* nephron is situated.   (4 marks)

7. Describe the role of the lungs in excretion.   (3 marks)

8. Figure 7.4 shows a section through the skin of a mammal.

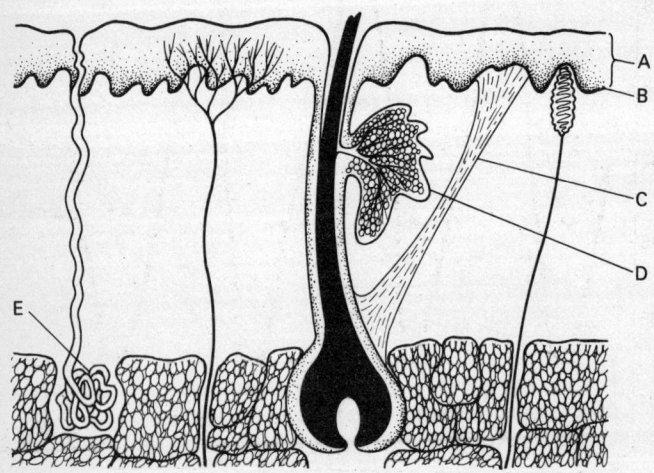

Fig. 7.4.

(a) Name the parts A–E.   (5 marks)
(b) Name two parts of the skin involved in temperature regulation.
                    (2 marks)
(c) What is the function of D?   (2 marks)
(d) The blood vessels in the skin are able to constrict and dilate. Under what circumstances do they do so and what effect does this have?
                    (4 marks)
9. Camels are well known for their ability to go without water for a long time. The graph in Fig. 7.5 shows the temperature variation in two camels. One camel was given water regularly, the other had not received water for a few days.
(a) Why is it important for mammals to maintain a constant body temperature?   (2 marks)
(b) Which camel shows the most daily variation in body temperature?
                    (1 mark)
(c) What does the graph tell you about the importance of water in temperature regulation?   (2 marks)

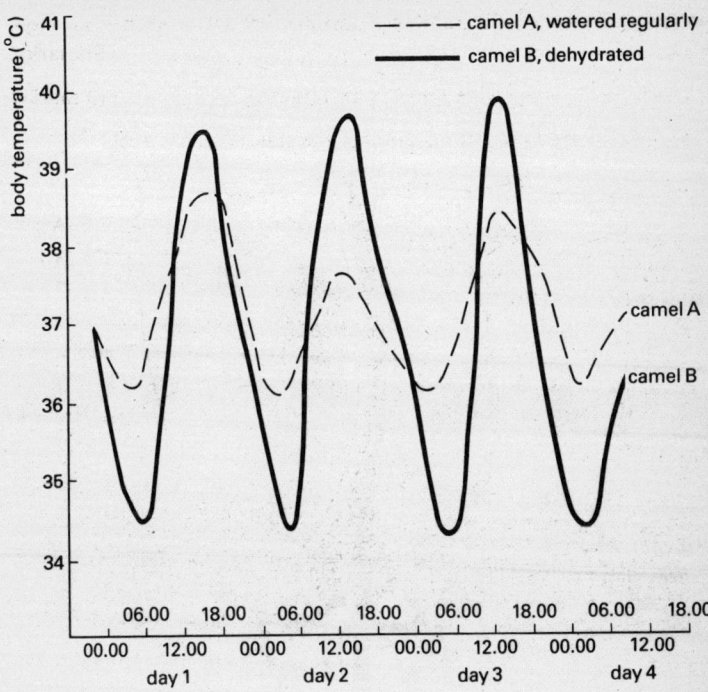

Fig. 7.5.

10. The average sweat production of a human is 500 cm³ per day. On a hot day this can rise to as much as 5000 cm³ per day.
(a) What changes would you expect in the composition of the urine on a hot day? (1 mark)
(b) Why can it be dangerous to sweat continually for long periods of time? (2 marks)
(c) What precaution can be taken by people who live in hot climates and sweat a lot? (1 mark)

11.
(a) How does *Amoeba* excrete nitrogenous waste? (1 mark)
(b) Why does an *Amoeba* living in fresh water need a contractile vacuole when an *Amoeba* living in sea water does not? (2 marks)

There are 60 marks for Section 2. If you were using books you should have got over 45 marks. 1 merit for 50 and over, 2 for over 55.

Section 3

Allow 25 minutes

1. The removal of the waste products of metabolism is called
   A. osmoregulation
   B. excretion
   C. egestion
   D. thermoregulation.   (1 mark)

2. Glucose and amino acids in the glomerular filtrate are reabsorbed from the
   A. collecting duct
   B. Bowman's capsule
   C. loop of Henlé
   D. first convoluted tubule.   (1 mark)

3.

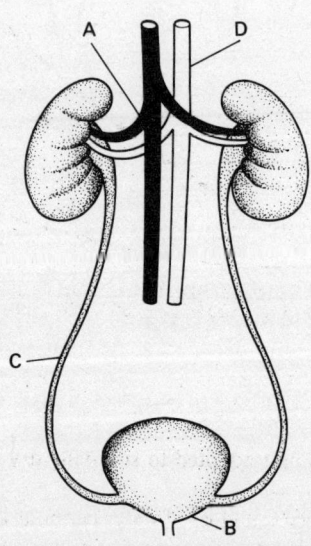

Fig. 7.6.

(a) Refer to Fig. 7.6 and complete the table.

Letter	Name	Function
	Renal artery	
C		
B		
		Carries blood from kidney

(8 marks)

(b) Describe the changes in the composition of the blood as it passes through the kidney. (5 marks)

4. Figure 7.7. shows the loss of water from two species of animal.

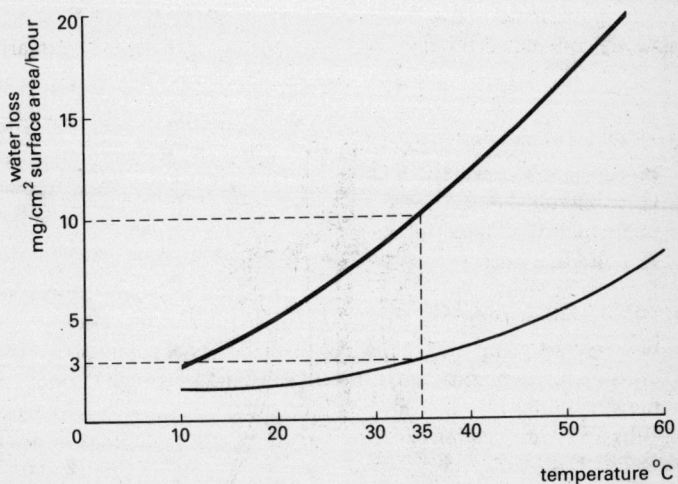

Fig. 7.7.

(a) Which animal is best adapted to surviving dry conditions?

(1 mark)

(b) What would be the total loss of water per hour for animals of species A and B if each has a surface area of 5 cm² and the temperature is 35 °C? (3 marks)

5. The table on p. 100 shows the organs responsible for removal of waste products from the body. Some of the table has been filled in for you. Try to complete it.

Excretory organ	Excretion	Excretory substances
Lungs	Expired air	(i)
(ii)	Urine	(iii), mineral salts
Skin	(iv)	(v)
Large intestine	Faecal matter	Nitrogenous substances
(vi)	Bile	Mineral salts

(6 marks)

There are 25 marks for Section 3. If you answered the questions from memory (which you should have done), over 15 is very good; over 20 is excellent.

Answers

Section 2

1. A   2. B   3. D   4. D   5. C   (1 mark each)
6.
(a) A. blood from renal artery
    B. Bowman's capsule
    C. glomerulus
    D. second convoluted tubule
    E. collecting duct
    F. loop of Henlé.   (6 marks)
(b) Ultrafiltration. Pressure builds up in the glomerulus because the blood vessel going into it is wider than the vessel coming out. This pressure forces plasma and dissolved substances through the walls of the glomerulus into the Bowman's capsule.   (2 marks)
(c) Salts and hydrogen ions are reabsorbed by active transport, water is reabsorbed by osmosis.   (2 marks)
(d) A lot of water is reabsorbed from the loop of Henlé. Desert mammals need to reabsorb a great deal of water, so the loop of Henlé is longer to provide a greater surface area for reabsorption.   (2 marks)
(e) Any two of these:
    water, urea, salts, modified hormones.   (2 marks)
(f)

Substance	Blood in A	Liquid in B	Liquid in E
Glucose	✓	✓	×
Urea	✓	✓	✓
Protein	✓	×	×

(9 marks)

(g)

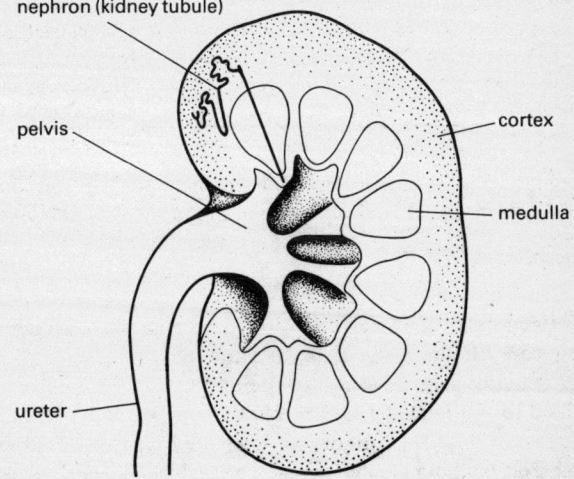

nephron (kidney tubule)

pelvis

cortex

medulla

ureter

Fig. 7.8. (4 marks)

7. Carbon dioxide and water are excreted from the lungs. Carbon dioxide diffuses from the blood into the alveoli and is then breathed out of the body. Exhaled air also contains water vapour which has vaporized into the alveolar air.

8.
(a) A. epidermis
   B. Malpighian (germinative) layer
   C. erector muscle
   D. sebaceous gland
   E. sweat gland. (5 marks)
(b) Any two of these:
   sweat glands, hairs, erector musles, surface blood vessels.
   (2 marks)
(c) D is the sebaceous gland which produces an oily fluid called sebum. Sebum keeps the epidermis and hairs supple and helps them repel water. It also contains an antiseptic which kills bacteria. (2 marks)
(d) On a hot day the blood vessels in the skin dilate, increasing the blood supply to the skin. Heat from the blood is therefore lost from the body more quickly. On a cold day the blood vessels in the skin constrict, reducing the rate of heat loss from the blood. (4 marks)

9.

(a) If mammals keep their body temperature constant the chemical reactions in the body work most efficiently because enzymes work best at an optimum temperature. This allows mammals to be active at most times of the year.   (2 marks)

(b) Camel **B**.   (1 mark)

(c) The graph shows that camels need to have water to regulate their body temperature efficiently. The dehydrated camel shows a wider range of temperatures because it does not have sufficient water to regulate its temperature as efficiently as the watered camel.

(2 marks)

10.

(a) The urine would be more concentrated because it would contain a lower proportion of water than on a cool day.   (1 mark)

(b) Sweat contains salts as well as water and urea. Continual sweating can lead to the loss of too much salt from the body. This would affect the osmotic pressure of the tissue fluid.   (2 marks)

(b) People living in hot climates can take salt tablets regularly to replace the salts lost in sweat.   (1 mark)

11.

(a) Nitrogenous waste from *Amoeba* diffuses out into the surrounding water by osmosis.   (1 mark)

(b) The cytoplasm of *Amoeba* is a stronger solution than fresh water. Hence an *Amoeba* living in fresh water needs a contractile vacuole to remove excess water. The cytoplasm of an *Amoeba* living in sea water is Isotonic (same concentration) with sea water. There is no uptake of water by osmosis so there is no need for a contractile vacuole.   (2 marks)

Section 3

1. B   2. D   (1 mark each)

3.

(a)

Letter	Name	Function
D	Renal artery	Carries blood to kidney
C	Ureter	Carries filtrate to bladder
B	Bladder	Stores urine
A	Renal vein	Carries blood from kidney

(8 marks)

(b) At the glomerulus the blood loses most of the plasma and the substances dissolved in it. Water, glucose, amino acids and salts are reabsorbed into the capillaries from the kidney tubule.

Blood leaving the kidney in the renal vein contains less urea and water than blood that enters it in the renal artery. If there is an excess of salts in the body, some of these will also have been removed from the blood.

4.
(a) Species B.   (1 mark)
(b) Show your working-out:
Species A at 35 °C loses 10 mg/cm^2 of water
For 5 cm^2, 10 × 5 = 50 mg of water per hour.
Species B at 35 °C loses 3 mg/cm^2/hr of water.
For 5 cm^2, 3 × 5 = 15 mg of water per hour.   (3 marks)

5.
(i) carbon dioxide, water; (ii) kidney and/or bladder; (iii) urea; (iv) sweat; (v) salts, water, urea; (vi) liver.   (6 marks)

8. Control and Coordination

It is for two reasons that organisms need some sort of coordination. Firstly, they need to be able to respond to stimuli from the environment. Secondly, the processes that go on in the body must work together to keep the organism functioning properly.

Section 1

Just a couple of questions done for you to get you in the mood.

QUESTION

1. (a) Name one hormone produced by mammals.   (1 mark)

Thyroid stimulating hormone.

(b) Where is this hormone produced?   (1 mark)

Pituitary gland.

(c) Which part(s) of the body does it affect?   (1 mark)

Thyroid gland.

(d) What effect does it have?   (1 mark)

Stimulates the production of thyroxine

2. Describe, step by step, what happens when a dog's bark is heard by a listener.   (15 marks)

When a dog barks the vocal chords vibrate, making the surrounding air

COMMENT

This sort of question can crop up in many subjects. You need to read the question through and make sure you can answer all of the parts about the hormone you name in (a).
There are many hormones you could name. I have chosen this one because its effects are localized. If you chose something like adrenalin your answers to (c) and (d) would have to be very long because adrenalin has a number of effects on many parts of the body.

Step by step means exactly what it says. You are expected to include as much detail as you can remember. As you can see, there is quite a lot of detail to be remembered!

molecules vibrate. These vibrations travel through the air and are directed into the listener's ear tube by the pinna. The tympanum is made to vibrate as a result. The vibrations are transferred through the middle ear by the ear ossicles (malleus, incus, stapes). When the stapes vibrates it moves the oval window, which in turn sets up vibrations in the perilymph of the cochlea. The endolymph then starts to vibrate, pulling the sensory cells in the organ of Corti. These sensory cells then send nerve impulses to the brain via the auditory nerve.

Whenever possible use the correct words.

Section 2

I expect you're raring to go now. Well here's your chance. There are no multiple choice questions this time so you can get straight down to the nitty gritty.

1.
(a) Distinguish between nastic and tropic responses in plants.

(2 marks)

(b) Give examples of positive and negative tropic responses.

(2 marks)

(c) Complete the table.

Tropism	Stimulus	Part of plant that responds positively
Phototropism	(i)	(ii)
(iii)	Gravity	(iv)

(4 marks)

2. Figure 8.1 shows a section through a human brain.
(a) Name parts A–E. (5 marks)
(b) State which part is involved in
    (i) the coordination of involuntary activities
    (ii) maintaining balance. (2 marks)
(c) Which of the structures is part of the endocrine system? (1 mark)

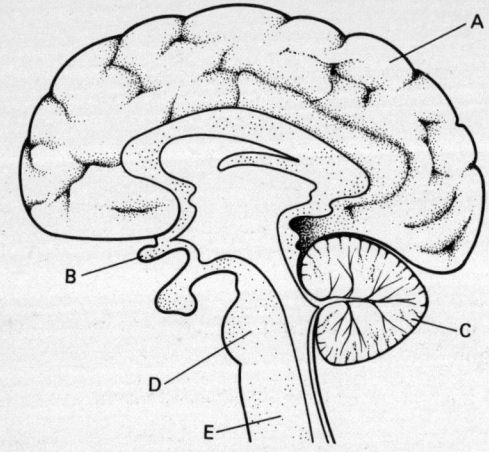

Fig. 8.1.

3. Figure 8.2 shows the middle ear of a mammal.

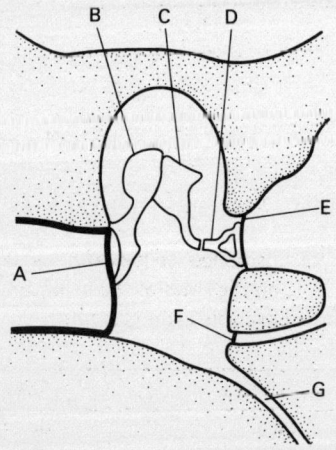

Fig. 8.2.

(a) Name parts A–G.   (7 marks)
(b) State which parts vibrate due to pressure changes in
    (i) the external auditory canal (ear tube)
    (ii) the cochlea.   (2 marks)

(c) Figure 8.3 shows an ampulla from one of the semi-circular canals.

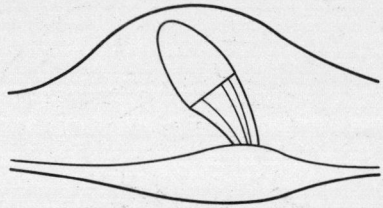

Fig. 8.3.

In which direction has the ampulla just been moved, left or right? Explain how you know. (2 marks)

4. Figure 8.4 illustrates one form of defective vision.

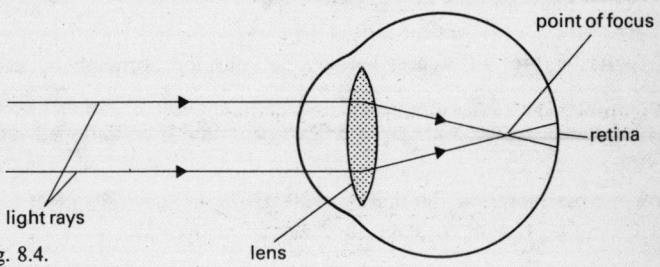

Fig. 8.4.

(a) What is this sort of defective vision called and what causes it? (2 marks)

(b) Explain, with the aid of diagrams, how it may be corrected by the use of spectacles. (4 marks)

(c) Cats have their eyes positioned at the front of the head, whereas rabbits have their eyes on the sides of the head. Explain why it is an advantage to each to have this arrangement. (4 marks)

(d) Complete the table.

Receptor	Stimulus	Sense
(i)	Light	(ii)
Ear	(iii)	(iv)
(v)	(vi)	Taste
Stretch receptors	Stretching	Muscle sense
Olfactory organs	(vii)	(viii)

(8 marks)

5. What do you understand by the following terms:
(a) grey matter   (2 marks)
(b) neurone   (1 mark)
(c) synapse   (2 marks)
(d) feedback mechanism   (3 marks)
(e) auxin   (2 marks)
(f) geotropism?   (2 marks)

6. Explain how light
(a) affects the diameter of the pupil in the mammalian eye   (2 marks)
(b) influences the direction in which seedlings grow   (3 marks)
(c) is focused on to the retina.   (3 marks)

7.
(a) Draw an outline of the human body showing the position of three
    endocrine glands.   (3 marks)
(b) Name one hormone produced by each.   (3 marks)
(c) How are hormones transported around the body?   (1 mark)
(d) Describe three differences between nervous and hormonal action.

                                                              (6 marks)

8. Distinguish between a simple reflex action and a conditioned reflex
action.   (2 marks)

Now it's marking time. 80 marks in all. Using books you should have
got 55 marks. 1 merit for over 60, 2 merits for over 70.

Section 3

Allow 30 minutes.
1. Figure 8.5 shows a section through a human eye.
(a) Which part of the eye is a layer containing rods and cones?

                                                              (1 mark)
(b) Name parts A and B and state the function of each.   (4 marks)
(c) In which part of the eye would you expect to find most cones?

                                                              (1 mark)
(d) Which part of the retina contains NO light-sensitive cells?

                                                              (1 mark)
(e) Draw a labelled diagram to show a section of the eye when cut along
    X–Y and viewed from the front.   (5 marks)
(f) Describe the changes that occur in a woman's eye when she looks up
    from a book she has been reading to look at a bird sitting on a
    distant tree.   (4 marks)

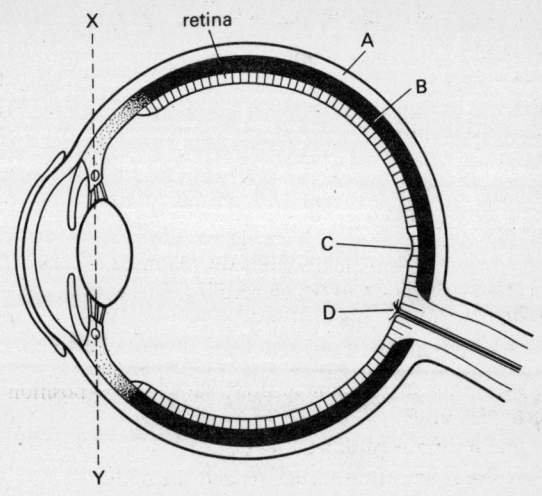

Fig. 8.5.

2. Describe the role of auxins in the response of a root to gravity.

(4 marks)

3. The table shows the effects of adrenalin on some organs of the mammalian body. Write appropriate answers for (a)–(j).

Organ	*Effects of adrenalin*	*Result of these effects*	*Effects on parts of body*
Heart	(a)	More glucose and oxygen available for muscles to use	(b)
Blood vessels of alimentary canal	Vessels constrict	(c)	Dry mouth, hollow feeling in stomach
Bronchus, lungs rib muscles and diaphragm	1. Relaxes tubes in lungs 2. (d)	(e)	(f)
Skeletal muscles	(g)	Ready for immediate action ('fight or flight').	(h)
Hair	(i)	Makes animal look larger and more frightening	(j)

(10 marks)

4. Match the words in the left-hand column to the appropriate description in the right-hand column. (10 marks)

(a) anti-diuretic hormone	(i) plant hormone
(b) hypothalamus	(ii) causes pupils to dilate
(c) clinostat	(iii) detects changes in blood temperature
(d) geotropism	(iv) controls the amount of light entering the eye
(e) iris	(v) response to gravity
(f) auxin	(vi) slowly revolving drum
(g) adrenalin	(vii) sensitive to vibrations
(h) organ of Corti	(viii) small gap between nerve cells
(i) synapse	(ix) seedling growth in response to lack of light
(j) etiolation	(x) stimulates water reabsorption from urine.

There are 40 marks for Section 3. Without books, 25 marks is good, 35 is very good.

Answers

Section 2

1.

(a) A nastic response is the movement of part of a plant which is *not* influenced by the direction of a stimulus. A tropic response is the movement of part of a plant which *is* determined by a stimulus.

(2 marks)

(b) The growth of a shoot towards a light is a positive tropic response. The growth of a shoot upwards away from the pull of gravity is a negative tropic response. (2 marks)

(c) (i) light; (ii) shoot or stem; (iii) geotropism; (iv) root. (4 marks)

2.

(a) A. cerebrum or cerebral hemisphere
   B. pituitary gland
   C. cerebellum
   D. brain stem or medulla oblongata
   E. spinal cord. (5 marks)

(b) (i) medulla oblongata
    (ii) cerebellum.   (2 marks)
(c) pituitary gland   (1 mark)

3.

(a) A. tympanum or ear drum
    B. malleus or hammer
    C. incus or anvil
    D. stapes or stirrup
    E. oval window
    F. round window
    G. Eustachian tube.   (7 marks)
(b) (i) tympanum or ear drum
    (ii) the organ of Corti.   (2 marks)
(c) The ampulla has moved to the right. This can be seen because, when
    the ampulla moves, the endolymph 'lags behind' briefly, pushing
    the cupula to one side.   (2 marks)

4.

(a) Short sight or myopia. This can be caused by the eyeball being too
    long or by the inability of the lens to change shape sufficiently to
    focus the light correctly.   (2 marks)
(b) Myopia can be corrected by using a concave (diverging) lens. This
    will refract light so it enters the eye at an angle that the eye lens can
    cope with.

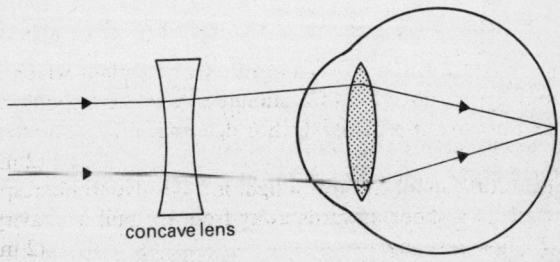

concave lens

Fig. 8.6.   (4 marks)

(c) The position of a cat's eyes allows it to have three-dimensional vision.
    This allows the cat to judge depth and distance when chasing its
    prey. Rabbits are a prey species and need to be continually alert to
    the danger of predators. Having their eyes on the sides of their heads
    gives rabbits a wide range of vision, allowing them to detect ap-
    proaching predators more easily.   (4 marks)

(d) (i) eye; (ii) sight; (iii) sound; (iv) hearing; (v) taste buds; (vi) chemicals in food; (vii) chemicals in air; (viii) smell.   (8 marks)

5.

(a) Tissue in the central nervous system containing cell bodies and dendrites of nerve cells.

(b) Nerve cell.

(c) A gap where nerve cells meet.

(d) When a hormone regulates its own rate of production by affecting the endocrine glands that produce it.

(e) A plant hormone that regulates growth.

(f) Growth of a plant in response to gravity.   (12 marks)

6.

(a) Bright light decreases the diameter of the pupil; dim light increases the diameter of the pupil.   (2 marks)

(b) The shoot of a seedling grows towards light. This is because more auxin is present on the shaded side of the shoot which makes that side grow faster. As a result the shoot bends towards the source of light.   (3 marks)

(c) Light is focused on to the retina by the lens. When viewing a close object the lens is a round shape and the ciliary muscles are contracted. When viewing a far object the lens takes on a flatter shape. This is achieved by the relaxation of the ciliary muscles.   (3 marks)

7.

(a) Figure 8.7 shows the position of the main endocrine glands. You need to show three of these to answer the question.   (3 marks)

(b) This answer should relate to the three glands shown in (a).

                        (3 marks)

(c) Hormones are transported in the blood.   (1 mark)

(d) Any three of the differences shown in the table.

Nervous	Hormonal
Electrical impulse along nerve fibre	Chemical in bloodstream
Rapid transmission	Slow transmission
Immediate response	Response usually slow
Short-lived response	Long-lasting response
Localized response	Usually widespread response

                        (6 marks)

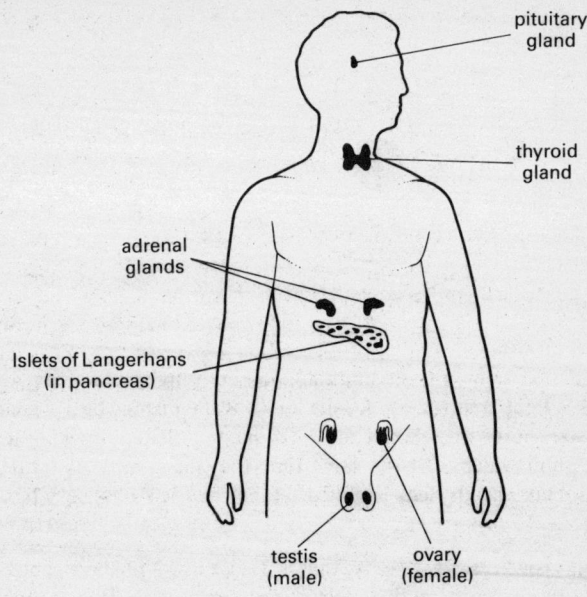

Fig. 8.7.

8. A reflex action is the immediate response to a stimulus which does not involve the brain for its initiation. In a simple reflex action the stimulus and response are related. In a conditioned reflex the original stimulus has been replaced by a different stimulus to produce the same response.

(2 marks)

Section 3

1.
(a) the retina. (1 mark)
(b) A. The sclerotic layer, maintains the shape of the eyeball.
    B. The choroid layer, prevents light being reflected inside the eye and contains the blood vessels which supply the eye.

(4 marks)

(c) The yellow spot or fovea (C). (1 mark)
(d) The blind spot (D). (1 mark)

(e)

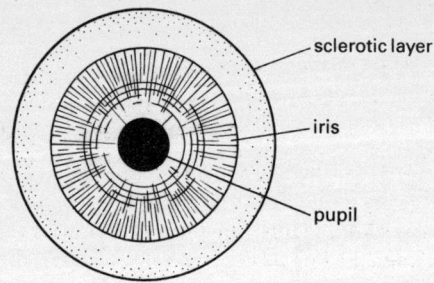

Fig. 8.8.   (5 marks)

(f) While the woman is reading the book her pupils are narrow and the lens is thick and round. As she looks at the distant bird the circular muscles in the iris relax, while the radial muscles contract. As a result the pupil widens. At the same time the ciliary muscles around the lens relax and the lens is pulled thinner by the suspensory ligament.
                                                                (4 marks)

2. Roots grow towards gravity; that is, they show a positive geotropism. In the root, auxins have the effect of slowing growth. It is thought that auxins move to the lower side of a root under the influence of gravity. As a result the upper side of the root grows faster than the lower side and the root grows downwards.   (4 marks)

3

(a) Heart beats faster.
(b) Blood is pumped around the body faster.
(c) More blood is made available to supply the muscles.
(d) Breathing rate increases.
(e) Oxygen is taken into the body faster.
(f) More oxygen is available for respiration.
(g) Blood vessels widen and the muscles receive more blood.
(h) Body shakes.
(i) Erector muscles contract.
(j) Hairs erect.   (10 marks)

4.

(a) and (x); (b) and (iii); (c) and (vi); (d) and (v); (e) and (iv); (f) and (i); (g) and (ii); (h) and (vii); (i) and viii); (j) and (ix).   (10 marks)

9. Support and Movement

This topic concerns both plants and animals, but most students tend to concentrate on animals. For this reason we will start with a plant question.

Section 1

QUESTION

1. Why do plants need to stand upright? Explain how this is achieved. (15 marks)

(*a*) *Leaves held high to catch sunlight*
(*b*) *Flowers held high. Insect pollinated flowers therefore more easily seen by insects. Pollen from wind-pollinated flowers is more easily caught by the wind.*
(*c*) *Fruits and seeds are more easily dispersed.*
(*i*) *The parenchyma* (*packing tissue*) *in the stem is made up of large rounded cells. When these are turgid they press against the epidermis of the stem and hold it rigid.*
(*ii*) *Some plant stems* (*e.g. sunflower and lupin*) *contain strands of cellulose which are strong and flexible.*
(*iii*) *Some cells in plant stems have a substance called lignin added to the cellulose in their cell walls. These lignified cells are wood. Some*

COMMENT

This is a difficult type of question because you have to plan the structure yourself.

First deal with the needs for a plant to stand upright.
These are the points you should mention, though of course you should write them out properly in essay form.

Now you can deal with how this is achieved. There are three factors which contribute to the strength of the stem.

wood is found in the form of fibres, while other wood is found in the walls of the xylem vessels. Wood helps to support the stem, particularly in shrubs and trees.

Section 2

1. Figure 9.1 shows the arrangement of some of the muscles and bones in the human leg.

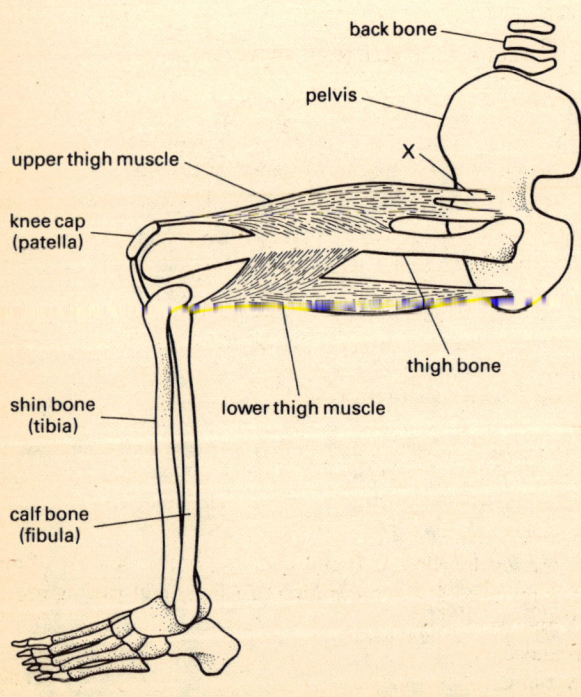

Fig. 9.1.

(a) Which muscle has just moved the leg into its bent position?

(1 mark)

(b) This muscle bent the leg by causing which bone to move?

(1 mark)

(c) While the leg was bending, what was the upper thigh muscle doing?

(1 mark)

(d) The part labelled X joins muscle to bone. What is it called?

(1 mark)

(e) What type of joint is found where the thigh bone meets the pelvis?

(1 mark)

(f) State two ways in which friction is reduced at this joint.

(2 marks)

(g) Which muscle is the flexor and which is the extensor? (2 marks)

(h) What is the word that describes the way these two muscles work together? (1 mark)

2. Figure 9.2 shows a fish seen from above.

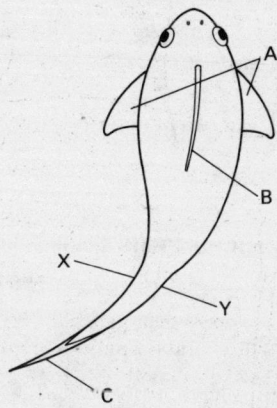

Fig. 9.2.

(a) Name the fins labelled A, B and C. (3 marks)

(b) The fins involved in the prevention of rolling and yawing are
   (i) A and B
   (ii) B and C
   (iii) A and C. (1 mark)

(c) Which paired fins are NOT shown in the diagram? (1 mark)

(d) If a muscle block at X contracts, what happens to a muscle block at Y? (1 mark)

3. Match the animals listed below with the appropriate type of skeleton.

(a) earthworm   (i) exoskeleton
(b) frog   (ii) hydrostatic skeleton
(c) locust   (iii) endoskeleton.   (3 marks)

4. The arrangement of a synovial joint is shown in Fig. 9.3.

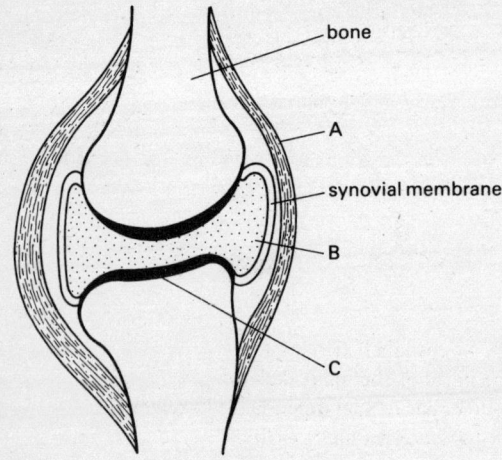

Fig. 9.3.

(a) Name parts A, B and C and state the function of each.   (6 marks)
(b) Name two places in the human body where synovial joints are found.   (2 marks)

5. State one way in which voluntary and involuntary muscle differ.

(1 mark)

6. Explain how birds are adapted to flight.   (12 marks)

40 marks for Section 2. It is quite an easy section so you need 30 marks for 1 merit mark, 35 or more for 2 merit marks.

Section 3

This is quite a short section so allow yourself 20 minutes.

1. Figure 9.4 shows the skeleton of a rabbit.

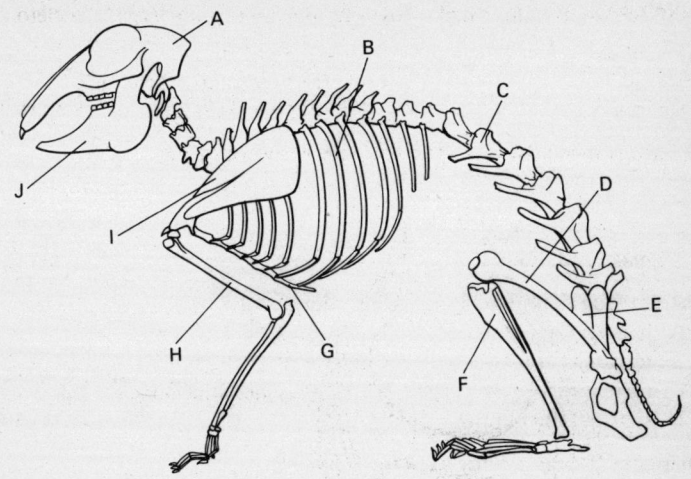

Fig. 9.4.

(a) Name the bones labelled A to J.   (5 marks)
(b) Name the parts of the axial skeleton.   (2 marks)
(c) Name four bones in the appendicular skeleton.   (2 marks)
(d) Where in the body would you find
    (i) a hinge joint
    (ii) a ball-and-socket joint
    (iii) a fixed joint?   (3 marks)
(e) Which muscle causes the front limb to bend?   (1 mark)

2. Figure 9.5 shows a land plant and a water plant.

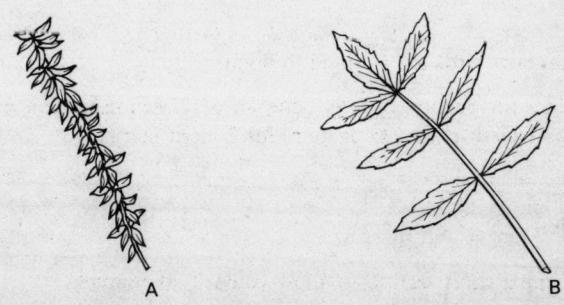

Fig. 9.5.

(a) Which is the water plant, A or B?   (1 mark)
(b) Why is there a difference between land plants and water plants?
                                                          (2 marks)
(c) Explain why plants wilt when they are short of water.   (2 marks)

3. The function of cartilage is to
   A. secrete synovial fluid
   B. hold bones together
   C. reduce friction
   D. make red blood cells.   (1 mark)

4. The tissue that attaches muscle to bone is
   A. ligament
   B. tendon
   C. cartilage
   D. synovial membrane.   (1 mark)

There are 20 marks altogether for Section 3.

Fun Time

The words listed below have had their letters mixed up. There is a clue
with each to help you rearrange them to find the answers.

1. LAPUSCA	shoulder blade
2. DONNET	connects muscle to bone
3. SPICEB	flexes the arm
4. MOSTOMEY	muscle blocks in fish
5. ANSOVILY	fluid found in joints

Answers

Section 2

1.
(a) Lower thigh muscle.   (1 mark)
(b) Tibia and/or fibula.   (1 mark)
(c) Getting longer and thinner.   (1 mark)
(d) Tendon.   (1 mark)
(e) Ball-and-socket joint.   (1 mark)
(f) Smooth shiny cartilage and synovial fluid.   (2 marks)

(g) Flexor = lower thigh muscle; extensor = upper thigh muscle.
(2 marks)

(h) Antagonistic. (1 mark)

2.
(a) A. Pectoral fins.
   B. Dorsal fin.
   C. Caudal fin. (3 marks)
(b) (ii). (1 mark)
(c) pelvic fins. (1 mark)
(d) It relaxes. (1 mark)

3. (a) with (ii); (b) with (iii); (c) with (i). (3 marks)

4.
(a) A. Ligaments. Hold bones together at joints.
   B. Synovial fluid. Acts as a lubricant to reduce friction between the bones of the joint.
   C. Cartilage. Smooth to reduce friction between the bones.
(6 marks)

(b) There are many synovial joints in the body, you only need to have 2. Obvious ones might be knee, elbow, shoulder or hip. (2 marks)

5. There are a number of possible answers:
Involuntary muscles contract less powerfully than voluntary ones.
The cells of involuntary muscle are unstriped and clearly separate from each other. Voluntary muscles are striped and the cells are not clearly separated from each other.
Contraction of involuntary muscles is not under conscious control; voluntary muscles are normally under conscious control. (1 mark)

6. To get your 12 marks for this question, there are twelve points you must mention. They are listed here, but you should present them in essay form:
Body is streamlined.
Feathers are contoured to smooth the outline.
The forelimbs are developed into wings.
Eyesight is very good so that food can be seen from high in the air.
The skeleton is made light by having many hollow bones.
The number of bones in the wings are reduced.
Some bones are fused to withstand stress.
Large keel on sternum for attachment of flight muscles.
Pectoral muscles are enlarged for flight.

No teeth, to reduce weight.
Efficient gas exchange system.
High body temperature for rapid metabolism.   (12 marks)

Section 3

1.
(a) A. skull (cranium); B. rib; C. vertebra; D. femur; E. pelvis; F. tibia;
    G. sternum; H. humerus; I. scapula; J. lower jaw.   ($\frac{1}{2}$ mark each)
(b) Skull, vertebral column, ribs, sternum.   ($\frac{1}{2}$ mark each)
(c) Any four of the bones not named above.   ($\frac{1}{2}$ mark each)
(d)   (i) Many possibilities; e.g. elbow, knee.
     (ii) Shoulder or hip joint.
    (iii) Fused bones of the cranium *or* joints between vertebrae and ribs
          or between sternum and ribs.   (3 marks)
(e) biceps.   (1 mark)

2.
(a) A.
(b) Water plants are supported by the water and do not need a strong
    stem to support themselves. Land plants have to support themselves
    and need a strong stem to do so.   (2 marks)
(c) When plants are short of water the cells of the parenchyma are not
    turgid and cannot hold the stem upright.   (2 marks)

3. C   4. B
                                                        (1 mark each)

Answers to Fun Time

1. SCAPULA
2. TENDON
3. BICEPS
4. MYOTOMES
5. SYNOVIAL

10. Reproduction

Organisms reproduce in a variety of ways; this chapter concentrates on mammals and flowering plants. You will find other groups of animals and plants mentioned in Chapter 14.

Section 1

QUESTION

1. Describe the structure of a NAMED, insect-pollinated flower. Explain how its structure is suited to its method of pollination. (10 marks)

COMMENT

To describe the structure the easiest way is to draw a diagram. NAMED is what it means and your diagram must look like the flower you have named. It must also be an insect-pollinated flower. Choose a simple structure – it is easier to remember and takes less time to draw.

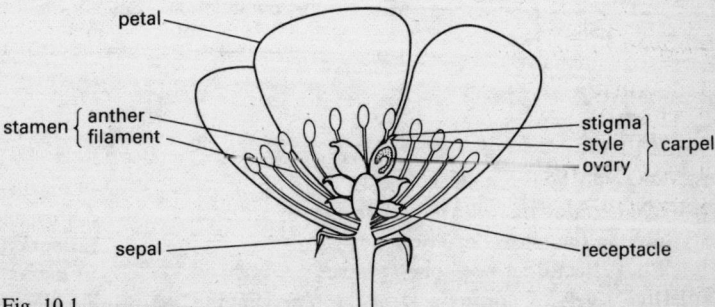

Fig. 10.1.

Flowers are large and conspicuous, often facing upwards so they are easily seen. The petals are brightly coloured to attract insects. Scent is also produced to attract insects.

Now you must describe the ways in which the flower is adapted to insect-pollination. These points are true for the majority of insect-pollinated flowers.

The stamens are positioned so that visiting insects pick up the sticky pollen on their bodies. The insect is guided to the nectar produced by the nectaries at the base of the petals by the honey guides on the petals.

Make sure you know the pollination details of the flower you choose. How the transfer of pollen is achieved varies from flower to flower.

An insect bearing pollen, when visiting another flower, may then transfer the pollen to the stigmas.

To prevent self-pollination the carpels do not ripen until the stamens are withered.

Methods of avoiding self-pollination should be mentioned if you know them.

Section 2

There are 60 marks for this section. Over 50 definitely deserves 2 merit marks, over 40 will just get you the one merit mark. If you get below 30 you have probably been too brief with your answers.

1. An outline of the menstrual cycle is shown below.

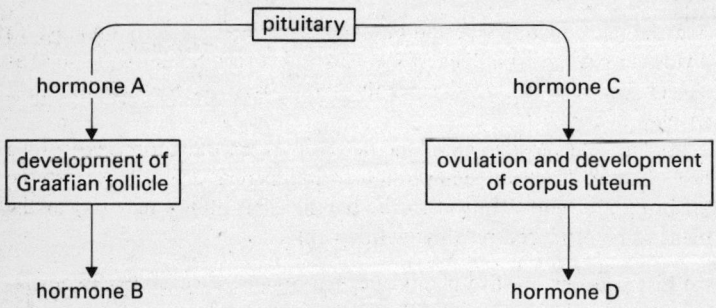

(a) Name hormones A, B, C and D.   (4 marks)
(b) What causes the release of hormone C while at the same time inhibiting the release of hormone A?   (2 marks)
(c) What effect does hormone D have?   (2 marks)
(d) High levels of hormone D in the blood inhibit the production of hormone C. Explain in detail what happens next.   (4 marks)
(e) What differences would there be if the ovum were fertilized?
                                                                   (3 marks)
(f) What role does the hormone oxytocin play in parturition?
                                                                   (1 mark)

2. An experiment was carried out to investigate the conditions necessary for germination. Seeds were exposed to different conditions and the results recorded as shown in the table.

Seeds	Conditions	Results
A	Dry, oxygen, light, 25 °C	No germination
B	Moist, no oxygen, light, 25 °C	No germination
C	Moist, oxygen, light, 5 °C	Germination slow
D	Moist, oxygen, light, 25 °C	Healthy seedlings
E	Moist, oxygen, dark, 25 °C	Long, spindly seedlings

Use the information in the table to list the conditions necessary for the germination and the production of healthy seedlings. Explain why each condition is necessary. (8 marks)

3.
(a) Use the words in the list to fill in the gaps in the passage.
(10 marks)

Genetically, simpler, Amoeba, binary fission, spores, identical, asexual, buds, change, generations.

Asexual reproduction is found in many plants and some (i) animals. (ii) divides into two (iii) individuals; this is called (iv). Some fungi, such as *Mucor*, produce (v). *Hydra* produces (vi) from its body wall. These develop into new *Hydra*.

In plants the most common method of (vii) reproduction is vegetative propagation. This can be important to commercial growers because the offspring are (viii) identical to the parent. This allows new (ix) of the plant to be produced reliably, without (x).

(b) Listed below are five plants and five organs of vegetative propagation. Match the organs with the appropriate plants (5 marks)

A. potato	(i) sucker
B. iris	(ii) bulb
C. onion	(iii) runner
D. rose	(iv) stem tuber
E. strawberry	(v) rhizome.

4. Figure 10.2 shows the structure of an oat flower.
(a) How is pollination achieved in oat plants? (1 mark)
(b) How is the structure of the flower limited to its method of pollination? (2 marks)

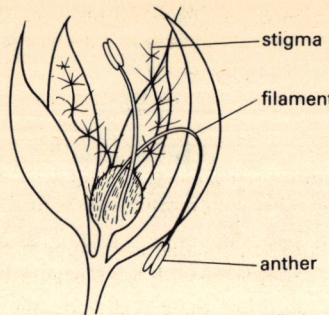

Fig. 10.2.

5. The reproductive systems of a human male and female are shown in Fig. 10.3.

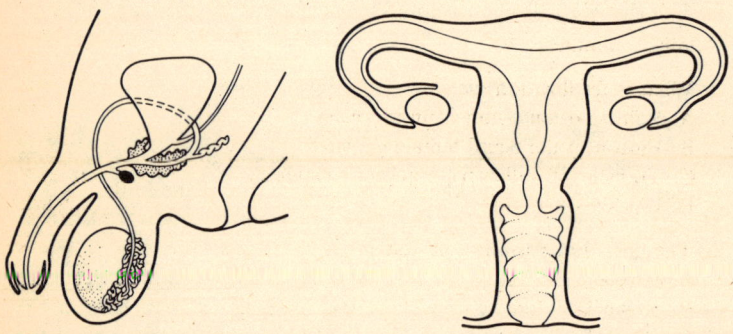

Fig. 10.3.

(a) Copy the diagrams (*you would not have to do this in an exam but it saves you writing in the book*) and label the following parts.

(4 marks)

Urethra, cervix, seminal vesicle, bladder, foreskin, uterus, prostate gland, vagina.

(b) On the diagrams mark with the letter indicated where the following activities take place: (5 marks)

    F. fertilization
    S. sperm production
    O. ova production
    I. embryo implantation
    T. sperm storage.

6. When two gametes fuse together at fertilization, the product is
   A. an ovary
   B. a spore
   C. a zygote
   D. an ovule. (1 mark)

7. How is the structure of the placenta suited to its role of allowing exchange of substances between mother and foetus? (3 marks)

8. A woman finds that she is unable to become pregnant even though she is having regular intercourse with her husband and they do not use any methods of contraception. Suggest the possible reasons for this.
(5 marks)

Section 3

Allow 30 minutes

1. What is fertilization?
   A. Release of an ovum from an ovary.
   B. Fusion of male and female gametes.
   C. Transfer of pollen from anther to stigma.
   D. Release of sperms. (1 mark)

2. The period of gestation in humans is
   A. 8 weeks
   B. 50 weeks
   C. 30 weeks
   D. 40 weeks. (1 mark)

3. Write down the *word* that best describes the following statements.
(10 marks)

(a) Scientific name for the womb.
(b) Ring of muscles at the base of the uterus.
(c) Release of an egg from the ovary.
(d) Seed coat.
(e) Formed from a flower's ovary wall.
(f) Produces pollen.
(g) Underground food storage organ of onion.
(h) Age at which production of sex cells begins in humans.
(i) Type of germination when cotyledons remain below ground.
(j) Sac containing the testes.

4. The fruits shown in Fig. 10.4 are adapted to different methods of seed dispersal. Explain how the structure of each fruit helps in the dispersal of its seeds.   (8 marks)

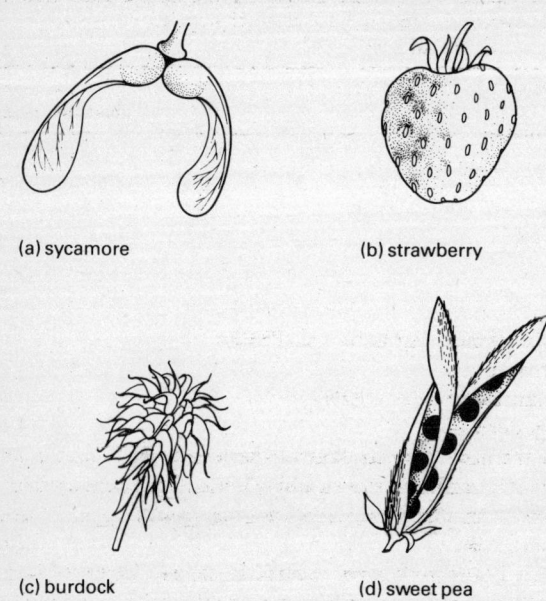

(a) sycamore

(b) strawberry

(c) burdock

(d) sweet pea

Fig. 10.4

5. The table shows a comparison between wind- and insect-pollinated flowers. Complete the table by giving the missing details.   (10 marks)

Characteristic	Wind-pollinated	Insect-pollinated
Whole flower	Small and inconspicuous	(a)
Position of flowers	(b)	Flowers face upwards
Petals	(c)	(d)
Nectar	None	(e)
Scent	(f)	Yes
Position of stamens and stigma	(g)	Stamens and stigma inside ring of petals

Characteristic	Wind-pollinated	Insect-pollinated
Number of pollen grains produced	Many	(h)
Type of pollen grain	Pollen grains light with smooth surface	(i)
Flowering time	(j)	Flowers open after the leaves in spring

Answers

Section 2

1.
(a) A. follicle stimulating hormone (FSH)
   B. oestrogen
   C. luteinizing hormone (LH)
   D. progesterone.   (4 marks)
(b) During the first fourteen days of the menstrual cycle the levels of oestrogen in the blood rise steadily. When they reach a certain level they cause the pituitary gland to stop producing FSH and start producing LH.   (2 marks)
(c) Hormone D (progesterone) controls the building up of the uterus wall ready to receive a fertilized ovum. Progesterone also continues the inhibition of FSH production and maintains the production of LH.   (2 marks)
(d) Inhibition of hormone C (LH) means that the corpus luteum is no longer stimulated to produce progesterone. This, in turn, leads to the breakdown of the thickened uterus walls, resulting in menstruation.
                                                    (4 marks)
(e) If the ovum were fertilized the pituitary would continue to produce LH. Consequently the corpus luteum would continue to produce progesterone. The presence of progesterone would maintain the wall of the uterus so that menstruation would not occur.   (3 marks)
(f) Oxytocin causes contractions of the uterus wall which leads to the baby being expelled through the vagina.   (1 mark)

2. Conditions for germination:
Oxygen – needed to make energy for growth.
Water – needed for reactions to take place in and to transport food to the growing parts.

Warmth – to provide correct temperature for enzymes to work.
Light – for photosynthesis by seedlings as food store in seed runs out.

(8 marks)

3.
(a) (i) simpler; (ii) *Amoeba*; (iii) identical; (iv) binary fission; (v) spores; (vi) buds; (vii) asexual; (viii) genetically; (ix) generations; (x) change.
(b) A with (iv); B with (v); C with (ii); D with (i); E with (iii).

(5 marks)

4.
(a) The pollen is carried by the wind from the anthers of one plant to the stigmas of another. (1 mark)
(b) The stamens hang outside the flower so that the pollen is easily caught by the wind. Similarly, the stigmas hang outside the flower and are feathery to increase the chance of pollen landing on them.

(2 marks)

5.

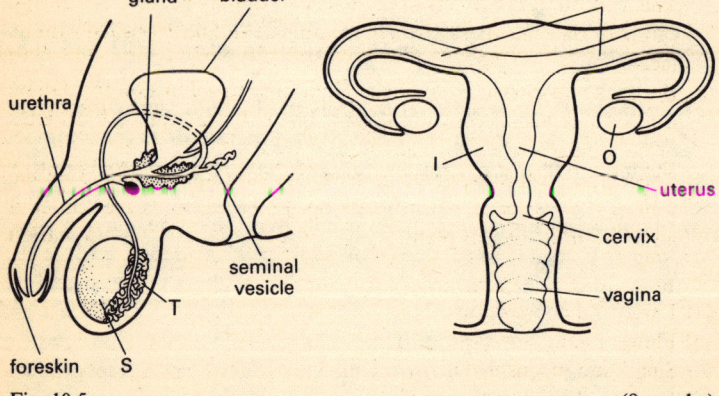

Fig. 10.5.   (9 marks)

6. C.   (1 mark)

7. The placenta is arranged so that a network of capillaries attached to the foetus come into close contact with blood spaces on the maternal side. This allows efficient exchange of substances between maternal and foetal blood. The villi of the placenta increase the surface area over which diffusion can take place.   (3 marks)

8. There are a number of things that can cause infertility. The male may not be producing any sperms or the sperms may not be formed properly. If the sperm duct is blocked, sperms will not reach the urethra, or the seminal fluid may not contain the chemicals necessary to activate the sperms. The female may not be producing ova, or the ova may not be properly formed. A blocked oviduct can prevent the ova meeting sperms. If the ovum is fertilized it may not be able to implant in the uterus wall properly.   (5 marks)

Section 3

1. **B**   2. **D**   (1 mark each)

3. (a) uterus; (b) cervix; (c) ovulation; (d) testa; (e) fruit; (f) anther; (g) bulb; (h) puberty; (i) hypogeal; (j) scrotum.   (10 marks)

4.
(a) Sycamore – dispersed by wind, helped by wing-like structures which catch the wind so that the seed is carried away from the parent plant.
(b) Strawberry – dispersed by animals. Fruit is fleshy and tastes good which encourages animals to eat it. The seeds may be scattered during eating or they may pass through the animal and be deposited with its faeces.
(c) Burdock – dispersed by animals. Hook-like structures on fruit allow it to be attached to fur of passing animals. It may then fall off later or be removed when the animal cleans itself.
(d) Sweet pea – self-dispersal. The seeds are contained in pods. As the wall of the pod dries out it bursts open and the seeds are scattered away from the parent plant.   (8 marks)

5.
(a) Large and conspicuous.
(b) Flowers hang downwards.
(c) Small and inconspicuous.
(d) Large and brightly coloured.
(e) Present.
(f) None.
(g) Stamens and stigmas hang outside ring of petals.
(h) Few.
(i) Pollen grains sticky or hooked.
(j) Flowers open before leaves in spring.   (10 marks)

11. Growth

Growth forms a relatively small part of the syllabuses, though the principles involved are very important.

There is only one section in this chapter. You may use books to answer the questions if you wish or you may attempt the questions under examination conditions. If you choose the latter, allow yourself 45 minutes. There are 45 marks; 1 merit mark for over 35, 2 for over 40.

Questions

1. Choose the best definition for growth.
   A. Increase in length of organism.
   B. Increase in mass of organism.
   C. Increase in protoplasm of organism.
   D. Increase in number of cells in organism.   (1 mark)

2. What is the best way to measure the growth of a gerbil? What are the disadvantages of this method?   (2 marks)

3. The table shows the increase in numbers of a colony of bees over a period of 100 days.

Days	0	10	20	30	40	50	60	70	80	90	100
Bees (*thousands*)	1	1·8	3·9	7	20	33	45	55	63	64	64·5

(a) Draw a graph to show the growth of the colony over this period.
                                                                  (4 marks)
(b) What starts to happen after about 80 days?   (1 mark)
(c) How do you explain this?   (2 marks)

4. The graph in Fig. 11.1 shows the increase in dry mass of an annual plant.

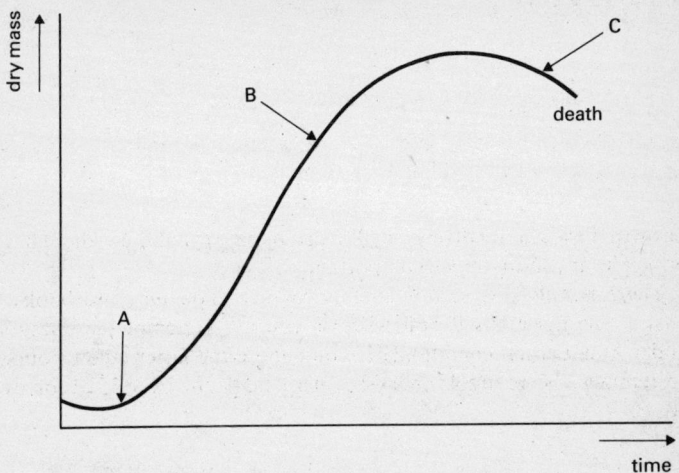

Fig. 11.1.

(a) What is happening at A, B and C? (3 marks)
(b) Describe, in detail, how you would investigate the rate of growth of seedlings. (4 marks)

5. The table below shows the development of different parts of the human body. The size of each part is given as a percentage of its final size.

Age (years)	Brain	General parts	Reproductive parts
2	51·0	24·0	3·0
4	78·0	40·0	8·0
6	88·0	48·0	9·0
8	98·0	50·0	9·5
10	98·3	52·0	10·0
12	98·7	56·0	10·5
14	99·0	70·0	11·0
16	99·2	83·0	32·0
18	99·7	96·0	65·0
20	100·0	100·0	100·0

(a) Draw a graph to show these results. (9 marks)
(b) Which parts of the body are growing fastest at the age of 2 years? (1 mark)

(c) Which parts of the body are growing fastest at the age of 17 years?
(1 mark)
(d) How do you explain these results? (3 marks)
(e) What sort of growth is shown in your graph? (1 mark)

6. In what ways are the life cycle of a butterfly and frog similar? What differences are there between these two types of life cycle?
(4 marks)

7. Figure 11.2 shows the life cycles of two insects, a housefly and a cockroach.

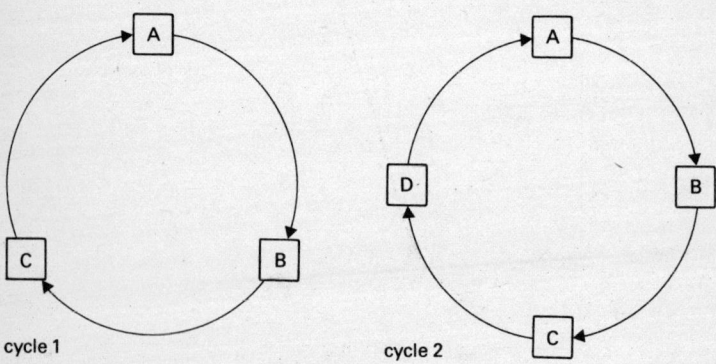

Fig. 11.2.

(a) Which cycle represents which insect? (2 marks)
(b) In each cycle, A represents the egg. Name the other stages shown for each cycle. (5 marks)
(c) What is the name of the growing stage in each cycle? (2 marks)

Answers

1. C. (1 mark)

2. By measuring the fresh weight of the gerbil at regular intervals its growth can be recorded. The disadvantage of this method is that it includes the water content of the gerbil. As this water content varies, the results may not be completely accurate. (2 marks)

3.
(a)

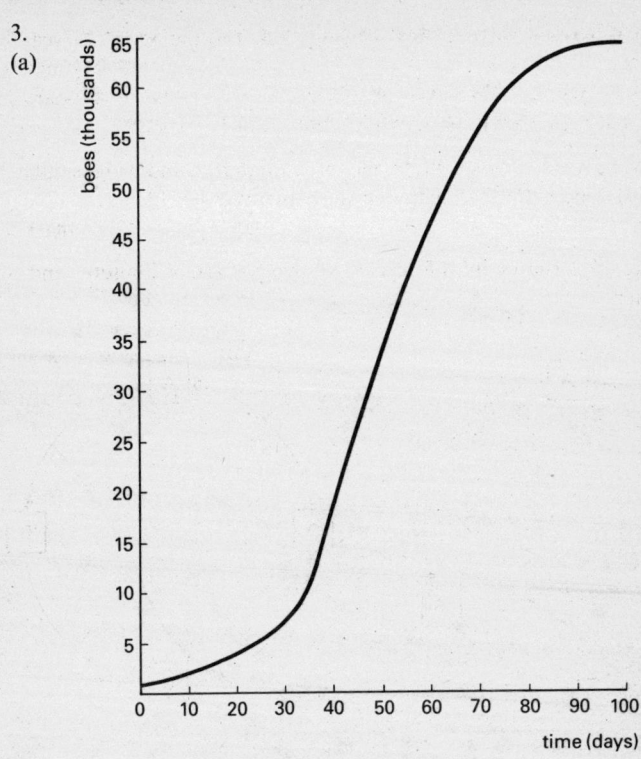

Fig. 11.3. (4 marks)

(b) After about 80 days the growth of the colony starts to level off.
(1 mark)

(c) Growth of the colony levels off because there is a limited amount of space and food available for the bees. (2 marks)

4.
(a) At A there is a slight decrease in mass because the seed's food store has been used up. At B the plant is growing steadily. The materials and energy for this growth are provided by photosynthesis. At C the mass decreases as a result of the loss of flowers and seeds.
(3 marks)

(b) To investigate the rate of growth of seedlings you would start by placing several hundred seeds under conditions in which germination should take place. Every few days, ten seedlings would be taken and heated at a steady 100 °C to remove the water. When dry, the seedlings are weighed and the overall weight is divided by ten to obtain an average dry weight. The average dry weight is recorded each time and eventually a series of dry weights indicating the rate of growth of the seeds is obtained. (4 marks)

5.

(a)

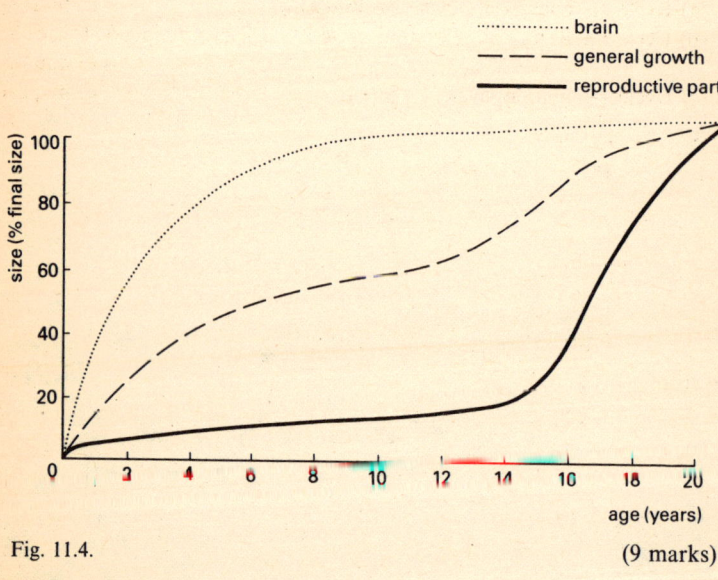

Fig. 11.4. (9 marks)

(b) The brain. (1 mark)
(c) The reproductive parts. (1 mark)
(d) The brain grows fastest because a young human has to develop coordination quickly in order to walk. The sense organs are also important from early on in life. The general parts of the body grow steadily until puberty, when there is a spurt of growth. The reproductive parts are not needed until puberty so they grow only slowly until that time. (3 marks)
(e) Allometric growth. (1 mark)

6. The life cycles of a butterfly and frog are similar in several ways. In both cases a larva emerges from the egg and the larva is *not* similar in appearance to the adult. The larva of both animals grows rapidly and

metamorphoses into the adult. There are also certain differences between the life cycles. The frog larva grows steadily and its development to the adult form is gradual. The adult continues to grow for some time before reaching sexual maturity. The butterfly larva grows in stages, each stage being separated by a moult of the cuticle. Metamorphosis takes place in the pupal stage, and the emerging adult is fully formed and sexually mature.   (4 marks)

7.
(a) Cycle 1 – cockroach; cycle 2 – housefly.   (2 marks)
(b) Cycle 1 – B. nymph, C. adult; cycle 2 – B. larva, C. pupa, D. adult.
                                                                    (5 marks)
(c) Cycle 1 – nymph; cycle 2 – larva.   (2 marks)

12. Genetics

Just the word 'genetics' strikes fear into the heart of many a biology student. It really isn't that bad though. Okay, there are lots of confusing words like heterozygote and homozygote, phenotype and genotype. The way to remember these is to try to understand what they mean. 'Hetero' always means 'different', so heterozygotes have different alleles of one gene. 'Homo' always means 'the same' (homogenized milk is the same throughout), so homozygotes have the same alleles of a particular gene. That leads us on to genotype. The 'geno' bit is a clue; it means what the genes are like. So phenotype must be the other one; that is, what the organism actually looks like.

As for working out crosses in genetics, well that's really a matter of practice. This chapter should give you plenty of that.

Section 1

This question is typical of the sort of question you will be expected to answer. It looks complicated at first, but is really quite straightforward, as you will see.

QUESTION

1. A red-coated bull was allowed to mate with a herd of cows. All of the cows had black coats and were of the same genotype. All of the resulting calves were black-coated.

(a) What genotypes were
   (i) the bull   (2 marks)
   (ii) the cows   (2 marks)
   (iii) the calves?   (1 mark)
Explain your answers fully.

COMMENT

Important information here, particularly the fact that all of the cows are of the same genotype.
As the calves are black, black must be dominant to red.

Let the allele for black coat be B, for red coat b.

(i) If B is dominant, then the genotype of the bull is bb as it has a red coat.

(ii) Black cows could be BB or Bb. If they were Bb, half of the calves would have a red coat. So the cows are BB.

(iii) From the above, it follows that the calves are Bb (heterozygotes).

If you decide this straight away it will save you a lot of writing. The recessive will only show in the homozygote bb.

cow \ bull	b	b
B	Bb	Bb
b	bb	bb

cow \ bull	b	b
B	Bb	Bb
B	Bb	Bb

(b) If the same bull was allowed to breed with the calves, what coat colours would you expect in the resulting offspring?   (2 marks)

If you worked out the genotypes correctly at first, this bit is then very easy.

bull bb, calves Bb

bull \ calves	B	b
b	Bb	bb
b	Bb	bb

The resulting offspring (F_2 generation) would be 50 per cent black and 50 per cent red.

Always show how you work things out. If you find it easier, work out which gametes are produced by each before drawing your table – but *do* show the examiner what you are doing.

(c) What offspring would you expect from a cross between a black bull and a red cow?
(4 marks)

Careful! Remember a black bull would be BB or Bb. The cow must be bb.

*Cow is bb, bull may be BB or Bb,
so there are two possibilities.
If the bull is BB:*

	b	b
B	Bb	Bb
B	Bb	Bb

All of the offspring are black.

If the bull is Bb:

	b	b
B	Bb	Bb
b	bb	bb

50 per cent of the calves will be black heterozygotes, 50 per cent will be red.

Or you could say there would be a 1 : 1 ratio of black to red calves.

(d) In some breeds of cattle, the gene for coat colour has alleles for red or white coat. These alleles are co-dominant and heterozygotes have a coat colour called roan. What colour would the calves be if a white bull were crossed with
  (i) a red cow   (2 marks)
 (ii) a roan cow   (2 marks)
(iii) a white cow?   (1 mark)

You may not always be told that alleles are co-dominant, but if you were told that red × white = roan it would be a bit of a give away.

Let the allele for red = R, and let the allele for white = W.

Again, state what symbols you are going to use.

(i) WW (bull) × RR (cow):

Part (d) is really just a matter of working methodically through each cross.

	R	R
W	WR	WR
W	WR	WR

All of the calves are roan.   WR must be roan.

(ii) *WW × WR:*

	W	R
W	WW	WR
W	WW	WR

50 per cent of the calves are white,
50 per cent are roan.

(iii) *WW × WW:*

	W	W
W	WW	WW
W	WW	WW

All of the calves are white.

Section 2

If you made sense of Section 1 you will find it easy to apply the same
procedures to that sort of question in this section and also in Section 3.

1. Meiosis occurs in
   A. the zygote of animals
   B. the root tip of plants
   C. the anther of plants
   D. the bone marrow of vertebrates.   (1 mark)

2. Meiosis always produces
   A. haploid cells
   B. diploid cells
   C. homologous pairs of chromosomes
   D. chromatids.   (1 mark)

3. Humans may have free ear lobes or fixed ear lobes. Free ear lobes (E) are dominant to fixed ear lobes (e). If two people with fixed ear lobes marry, the chance of them having children with fixed ear lobes is:

A. 25%

B. 50%

C. 75%

D. 100%   (1 mark)

4. Figure 12.1 shows one stage of mitosis.

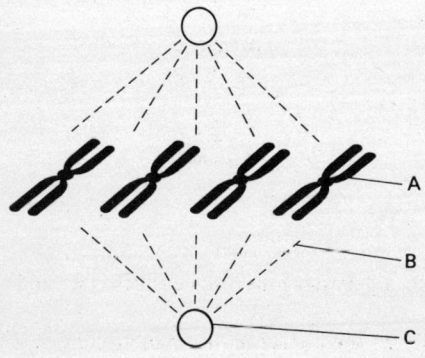

Fig. 12.1.

(a) Name the structures labelled A, B and C.   (3 marks)
(b) What happens during the next stage of mitosis?   (1 mark)
(c) What is the diploid number of chromosomes for this cell?

                                                                         (1 mark)

5. The diploid number of chromosomes in a human cell is 46. Some of the stages leading to the development of an adult human are shown in Fig. 12.2.
State how many chromosomes would be found in the cells at each stage.
                                                                         (7 marks)

6. A woman belonging to blood group B claimed that a man of blood group AB was the father of her child. The child was of blood group O. Could the man have been the father?
What was the genotype of the mother?   (2 marks)

7. Some people are able to roll their tongue while others cannot. Tongue rolling is due to a dominant allele, R. A homozygous tongue roller has

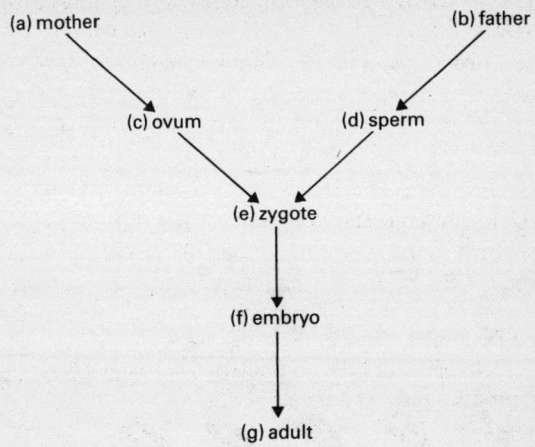

Fig. 12.2.

the genotype RR, a heterozygous tongue roller is Rr and a homozygous non-roller is rr.

Figure 12.3 shows the incidence of tongue rolling in a family.

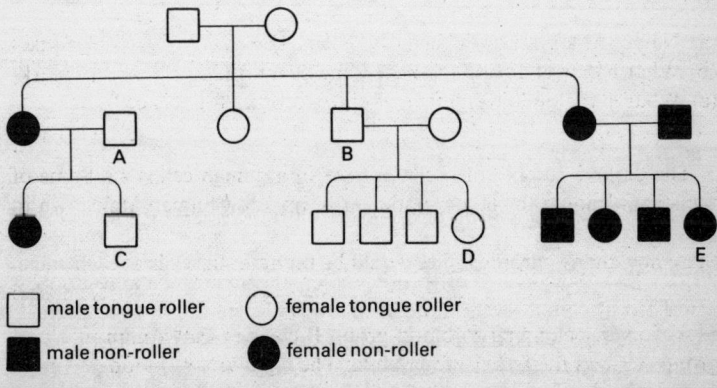

Fig. 12.3.

State the possible genotypes of persons, A, B, C, D and E, giving your reasons.
(10 marks)

8. In mice, the allele for brown coat colour, B, is dominant to that for white coat colour, b.

A mouse called Eric was crossed with 10 female brown mice. All of the offspring (the F_1 generation) were brown. When the F_1 generation were bred among themselves (selfed) the F_2 generation contained 303 brown mice and 106 white mice. What colour was Eric? Explain how you know. (4 marks)

9. Warfarin is a poison that was once used to kill rats. In most areas rats are now resistant to this poison. The allele for resistance, w, is recessive to the normal allele, W. In an experiment 50 rats were allowed to breed among themselves and their 400 offspring were fed with Warfarin. 95 of the offspring survived. Explain these results. (3 marks)

10. Figure 12.4 represents the combination of gametes of a man and woman to produce three children.

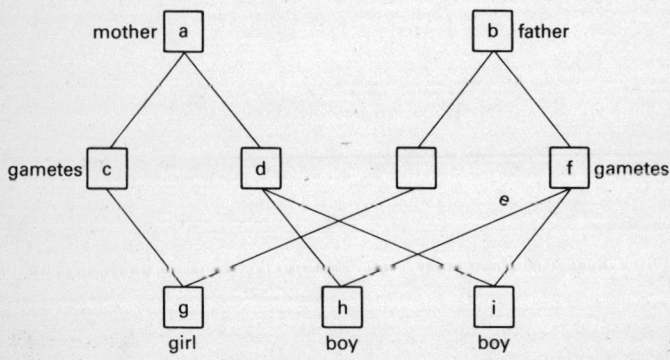

Fig. 12.4.

For each stage, labelled a–i, state which of the sex chromosomes would be present. (9 marks)

11. Mules are the hybrid offspring of a female horse and a male donkey. Until recently mules were thought to always be sterile. In 1981 a female mule gave birth to a foal, much to the surprise of scientists. The passage below is taken from the magazine *New Scientist*. Read the passage carefully and answer the questions that follow.

The mother died in 1983 but analysis of her chromosomes showed that she was without doubt a hybrid. In particular, her two X-chromosomes were clearly one of horse and one of donkey. Her offspring, called

Dragon Foal, had 62 chromosomes, the same number as a donkey, and both of her X-chromosomes were donkey. Her sire was assumed to be the donkey familiar with her mother, so she had a complete set of donkey chromosomes but she also had several *paired* donkey chromosomes. The conclusion is that she received the paired chromosomes from her mother. The mother also contributed some horse chromosomes to her foal.

Interestingly, Dragon Foal looks more like a chimaera than a hybrid. That is, she shows a patchwork of horse, donkey and mule characteristics – rather than a blend.

(a) Name one piece of evidence that shows the mother was definitely a hybrid.   (1 mark)

(b) In what ways were Dragon Foal's chromosomes similar to those of a donkey?   (2 marks)

(c) How did Dragon Foal acquire some horse chromosomes?
                                                                         (1 mark)

(d) How many Y-chromosomes would you expect Dragon Foal to have?
                                                                         (1 mark)

(e) What is a chimaera?   (1 mark)

(f) What difference was there between the X-chromosomes of Dragon Foal and those of her mother?   (1 mark)

There are 50 marks for this section. You certainly deserve 1 merit mark for getting over 40, 2 merits for over 45.

Section 3

Allow yourself 30 minutes to tackle these questions. There are 25 marks available to you; all you have to do is earn them.

1. As a result of meiosis:
    A. two nuclei are formed, each with half the original number of chromosomes
    B. two nuclei are formed, each with the original number of chromosomes
    C. four nuclei are formed, each with the original number of chromosomes
    D. four nuclei are formed, each with half the original number of chromosomes.   (1 mark)

2. In the fruit fly *Drosophila* normal wing D is dominant to dumpy wing d. If a heterozygous, normal winged fly is crossed with a dumpy winged fly the offspring will be
   A. all dumpy winged
   B. half normal winged, half dumpy winged
   C. all normal winged
   D. quarter dumpy winged, three-quarters normal winged.   (1 mark)

3. Figure 12.5 shows the nucleus of a cell before meiosis.

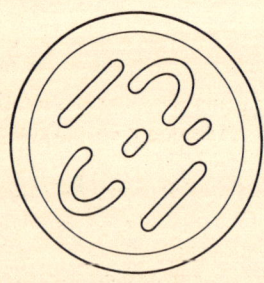

Fig. 12.5

(a) Draw a nucleus of a cell from the same species of organism after meiosis.   (2 marks)
(b) Where would you find meiosis occuring in a human male?

(1 mark)

4. In some parts of England there are two varieties of the peppered moth *Biston betularia*. The melanic or dark variety is dominant to the light variety.

When a melanic moth was crossed with a light coloured moth all of the F_1 generation were melanic. The F_1 generation were then selfed (crossed with each other) and the resulting F_2 generation contained 75 per cent melanic moths and 25 per cent light moths.

Using the symbols, M for melanic and m for light, state whether the following statements are true or false.

(a) The genotype of the original light moth was mm.   (1 mark)
(b) The original melanic parent was heterozygous.   (1 mark)
(c) Crossing the F_1 moths with light moths would result in the same proportions of offspring as seen in the F_2 generation described.

(1 mark)

(d) To discover which of the F_2 melanic moths were heterozygous you would back-cross to an mm moth.   (1 mark)

5. Albinism (being albino) in humans is caused by a recessive gene which we will call a.
(a) How can normal parents produce albino children?   (2 marks)
(b) If a couple have had one albino child, what is the chance of their second child also being albino?   (2 marks)
(c) What is the genotype of an albino?   (1 mark)

6. Explain the meanings of the following terms:
(a) phenotype
(b) genotype
(c) hybrid
(d) mutation.   (4 marks)

7. The coats of guinea pigs may be rough or smooth. When a rough-coated guinea pig was crossed with a smooth-coated guinea pig all of the offspring had rough coats.
(a) Which is the dominant allele, rough or smooth?   (1 mark)
(b) Using the symbols G and g, state the genotypes of the parent guinea pigs and the F_1 guinea pigs.   (3 marks)
(c) What would the offspring from a cross between two of the F_1 guinea pigs be like?   (3 marks)

Answers

Section 2

1. C   2. A   3. D   (1 mark each)

4.
(a) A. chromosome
   B. spindle
   C. centriole.   (3 marks)
(b) The chromatids of each chromosome move apart, going to opposite poles of the spindle.   (1 mark)
(c) 4.

5.
(a) 46; (b) 46; (c) 23; (d) 23; (e) 46; (f) 46; (g) 46.

6. No, the man could not have been the father. The genotype of the mother was BB.   (2 marks)

7.

A is Rr because one of his children is rr. If he was RR all of his children would be Rr.   (2 marks)

B could be RR or Rr. You cannot say which because the genotype of his wife is not known.   (2 marks)

C must be Rr because his mother is rr; therefore he must inherit one r from her.   (2 marks)

D could be RR or Rr.   (2 marks)

E is rr because he is a homozygous non-roller, and all non-rollers are rr.
                                                            (2 marks)

8. Eric was white. You can work this out by working back from the F_2 generation. In the F_2 there is approximately a 3:1 ratio of brown to white. This ratio can only occur by crossing heterozygotes Bb; i.e. Bb × Bb:

brown : white

	B	b
B	BB	Bb
b	Bb	bb

So, all of the F_1 mice were Bb. The only cross that will produce all Bb is BB × bb:

all heterozygotes

	b	b
B	Bb	Bb
B	Bb	Bb

We know that the females were brown, so Eric must have been white.

9. Approximately one-quarter of the rats survived. This means that the incidence of non-resistance to resistance in the F_1 generation was 3:1. To obtain this result, the parent rats must have been heterozygous, Ww.
                                                            (3 marks)

10.
(a) XX; (b) XY; (c) X; (d) X; (e) X; (f) Y; (g) XX; (h) XY; (i) XY.

(9 marks)

11.
(a) Her X-chromosomes were one of horse and one of donkey.

(1 mark)
(b) Dragon Foal has the same number of chromosomes as a donkey and both her X-chromosomes are donkey. (2 marks)
(c) She received them from her mother. (1 mark)
(d) Dragon Foal would not have any Y-chromosomes because they are only found in males. (1 mark)
(e) A chimaera is a patchwork of characteristics of different species rather than a blend. (1 mark)
(f) Dragon Foal's X-chromosomes were both donkey, whereas her mother had one of horse and one of donkey. (1 mark)

Section 3

1. D   2. B   (2 marks)
3.
(a)

Fig. 12.6.   (2 marks)

(b) In the testes.   (1 mark)
4.
(a) true; (b) false; (c) false; (d) true.   (4 marks)
5.
(a) The only way normal parents could produce an albino child is if both parents are heterozygotes, Aa. (2 marks)

(b) As the couple have had one albino child they must both be heterozygous.

	A	a
A	AA	Aa
a	Aa	aa

1 child in 4 could be albino, so there is a 25 per cent chance of their next child being albino. (2 marks)

(c) The genotype of an albino is aa. (1 mark)

6.

(a) Phenotype – the observable characteristic of an organism resulting from its genotype. (1 mark)

(b) Genotype – the genetic constitution of an individual. (1 mark)

(c) Hybrid – an organism which results from a cross between two parents that are genetically unlike. (1 mark)

(d) Mutation – a sudden change in the amount or structure of chromosomal material. (1 mark)

7.

(a) Rough coat is dominant. (1 mark)

(b) Rough-coated parent GG; smooth-coated parent gg; F_1 guinea pigs Gg. (3 marks)

(c) If the F_1 were selfed (Gg × Gg):

	G	g
G	GG	Gg
g	Gg	gg

In the resulting F_2 guinea pigs, 75 per cent would be rough coated, 25 per cent would be smooth coated. Of the rough-coated guinea pigs, two-thirds would be heterozygotes, one-third would be homozygotes.

(3 marks)

13. Ecology

Ecology is a wide-ranging subject and the detail you are required to know varies between syllabuses. All of the examination boards, however, require you to know about certain areas of ecology. You will be answering questions on these topics in this chapter.

Section 1

Most of the topics in this chapter tend to come up as short or structured questions. Very often they require you to interpret a graph or histogram:

QUESTION   COMMENT

1. DDT is an insecticide that was once used widely in Britain. Its use

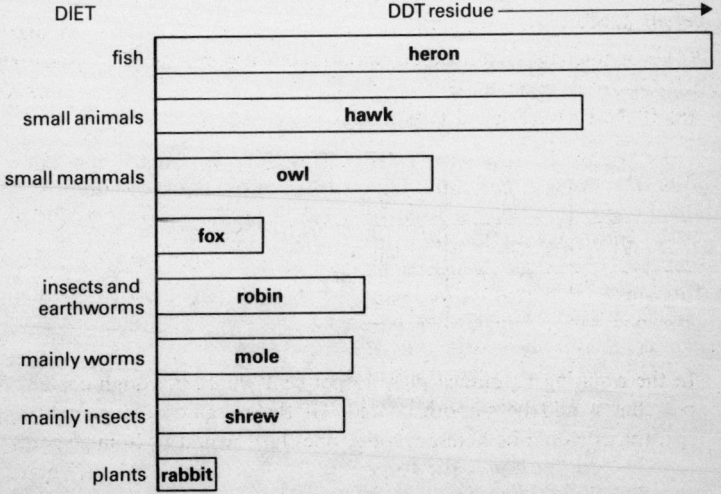

Fig. 13.1.

was eventually banned because of the way it accumulated in other animals. Figure 13.1 shows the relative amounts of DDT residue that might be found in a number of animals.

(a) DDT was used mainly on agricultural land. How did it find its way into herons?   (3 marks)

DDT applied to farmland gets washed into nearby water. From the water, it gets into fish. The heron obtains the DDT by eating the fish.

(b) Why do you think the herons receive such a large dose of DDT compared to the other animals?
    (3 marks)

Most of the DDT sprayed on to land goes into the soil. Therefore large quantities of DDT are washed into water and taken up by fish. Because of this the heron is exposed to relatively more DDT than an animal eating insects.

(c) Why do hawks receive a greater dose of DDT than shrews?
    (3 marks)

Shrews receive most of their DDT from the insects they eat. Each insect contains a small amount of DDT, but as shrews eat many insects they receive quite a large dose. Hawks eat small animals, including shrews. If each of these small animals contains a fairly large amount of DDT and a hawk eats a lot of them, it will receive a much greater dose.

(d) What do you think the foxes ate mainly? Explain your answer.   (3 marks)

Notice that herons feed on fish, so the DDT must get to the fish.

If you know about leaching of minerals from soils, it follows that DDT can get to water in the same way.

This takes a bit of thinking about. It is clear that soil in a field covers a larger area than the insects in the field. Therefore more spray will hit the soil than hits the insects. If it hits plants it will be washed off them and into the soil.

This follows from your knowledge of pyramids of numbers.

Foxes had a lower dose of DDT than the other secondary consumers. This suggests that foxes fed mainly on animals which themselves had a low dose of DDT. In this case it is probably rabbits.

This is fairly logical if you think about it.

Section 2

There are seven questions in this section for you to have a go at, with 45 marks available. Over 35 marks will get you one merit mark while over 40 marks will earn you the princely sum of 2 merit marks.

1. Figure 13.2 shows part of the energy flow through the environment.

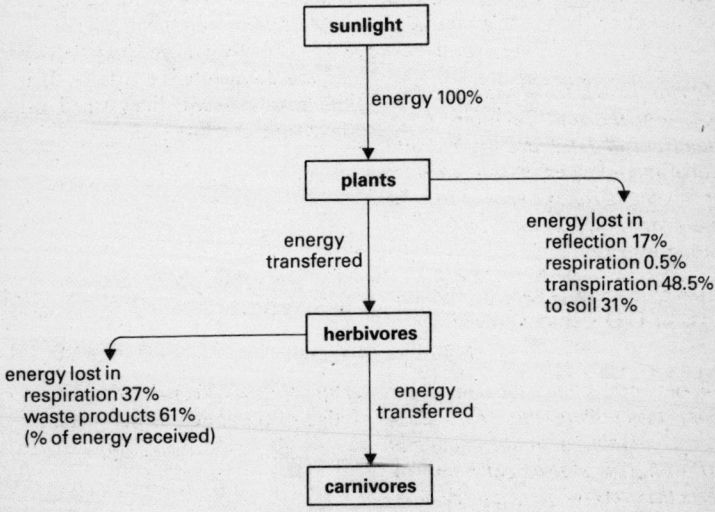

Fig. 13.2.

(a) How much energy (%) is transferred from: (i) plants to herbivores; (ii) herbivores to carnivores? (2 marks)
(b) Of the type of organisms shown, which are: (i) the producers; (ii) the consumers? (2 marks)
(c) If the herbivores received 200 kilojoules (kJ) of energy from the plants, how much energy would be used up in respiration by the herbivores? (2 marks)

2. Look carefully at Fig. 13.3 before attempting the questions.
(a) Name a suitable compound for (i) to (v).   (5 marks)
(b) By what process does compound (v) lead back to compound (i)?
                                                      (1 mark)

(c) What cycle does the diagram represent?   (1 mark)

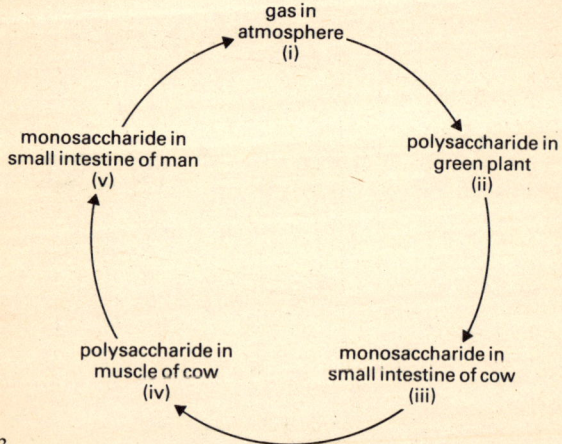

Fig. 13.3.

3. Figure 13.4 shows the main parts of the water cycle. State what is happening to the water at each of the stages a to h.   (8 marks)

4. The pyramid of numbers for a three-stage food chain is shown in Fig. 13.5.

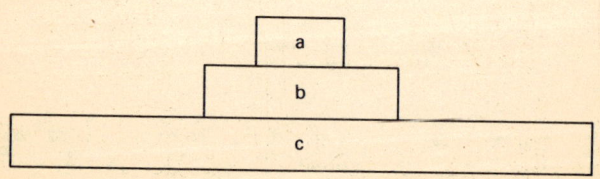

Fig. 13.5.

State which stage (a, b or c) represents each of the following: hawk; seeds; sparrow.   (3 marks)

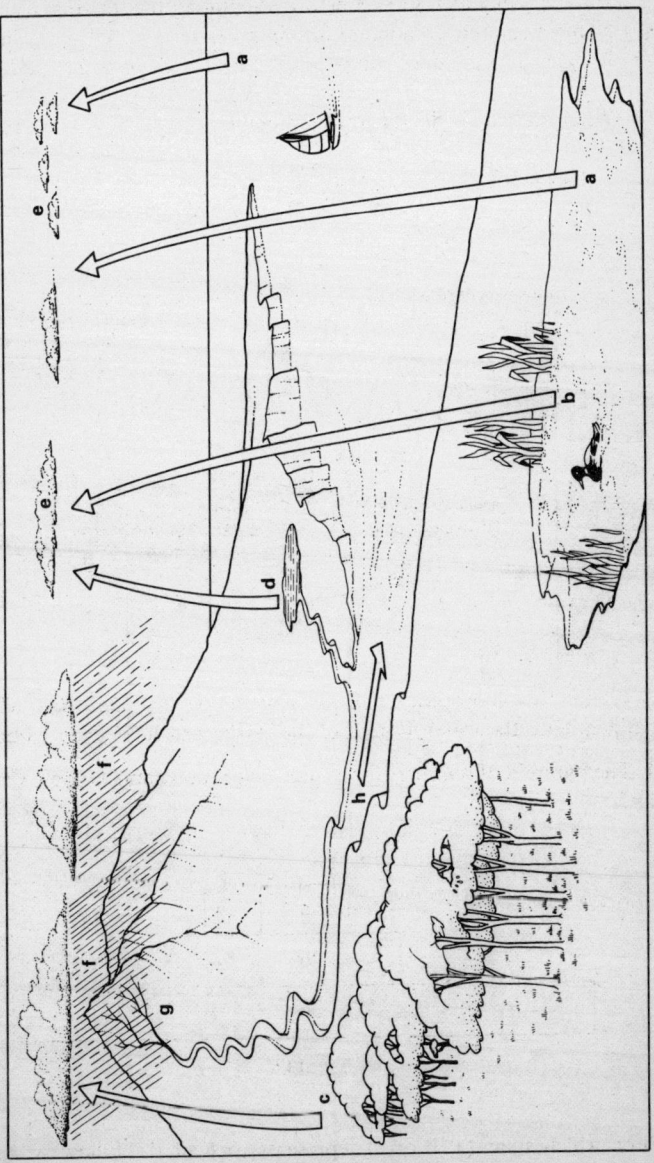

Fig. 13.4.

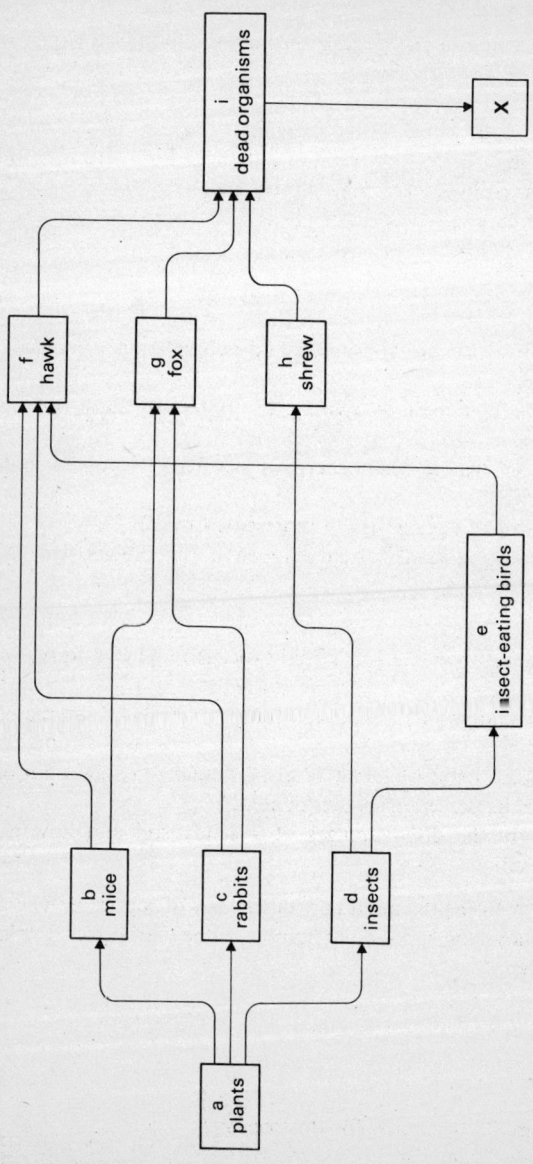

Fig. 13.6.

5. Look carefully at the food web shown in Fig. 13.6.

(a) The direction of energy flow through the food web would be
   A. a, d, e, f
   B. a, c, h, i
   C. h, e, d, a
   D. i, g, b, a.   (1 mark)

(b) Biomass will increase in which sequence?
   A. a, d, h, g
   B. g, h, d, i
   C. f, e, d, a
   D. h, g, b, a   (1 mark)

(c) Name two primary consumers and two secondary consumers from this food web.   (2 marks)

(d) List one food chain containing four organisms from this web.
                                                               (1 mark)

(e) Name one way in which energy is lost from the food web.
                                                               (1 mark)

(f) What sort of organisms are represented by X?   (1 mark)

(g) What do you think would happen if the rabbits were killed by disease?   (2 marks)

6.
(a) List the components you would expect to find in a fertile soil.
                                                               (3 marks)

(b) How would you determine the water content of a sample of soil?
                                                               (2 marks)

(c) A sample of soil weighing 20 g was found to contain 5 g of water. What is its percentage water content?   (1 mark)

(d) What are the disadvantages of a sandy soil and how can it be improved?   (4 marks)

7. Species A forms the main part of the diet of species B. The graph in Fig. 13.7 shows the variation in number of the two species. Explain what is happening.   (2 marks)

Section 3

Allow yourself 30 minutes for this section.

1. Figure 13.8 shows the general arrangement of part of a food web.

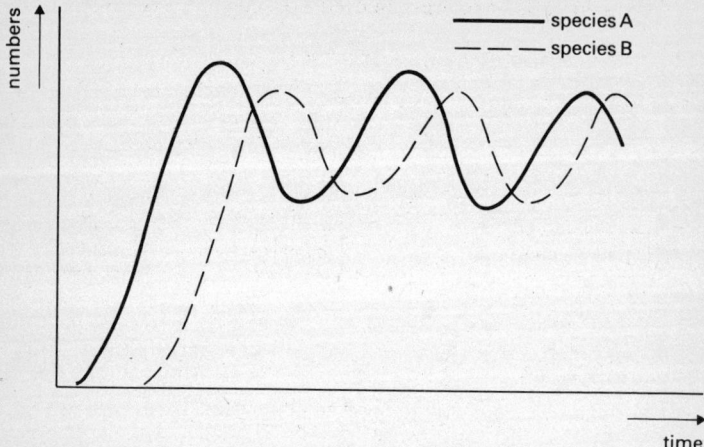

Fig. 13.7.

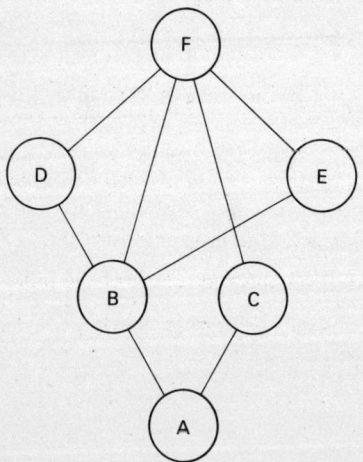

Fig. 13.8.

(a) What would happen to C if B was wiped out?   (2 marks)
(b) What would happen to F if C was removed from the food web?
(1 mark)

2. The main parts of the carbon cycle are shown in Fig. 13.9.

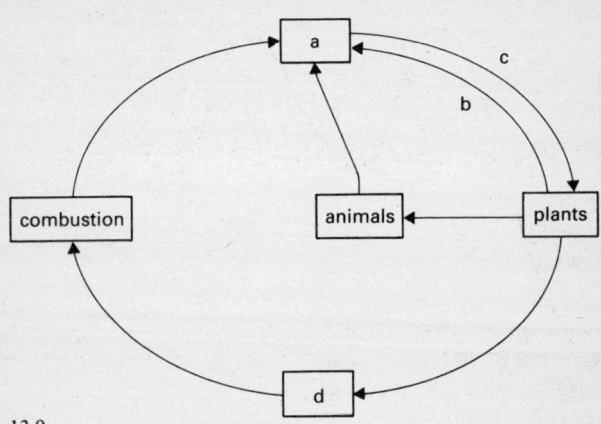

Fig. 13.9.

Name a, b, c and d. (4 marks)

3. The terms listed below are components of the nitrogen cycle:

atmospheric nitrogen   nitrite
plant protein   nitrate bacteria
nitrite bacteria   animal protein
nitrogen-fixing bacteria   ammonium.
denitrifying bacteria

(a) Use these terms to draw a diagram of the nitrogen cycle.

(9 marks)

(b) Why is clover important in crop rotation? (1 mark)

4. Draw a pyramid of numbers to represent the following food chain:

grass → snails → thrushes → sparrow hawk. (3 marks)

There are 20 marks for Section 3.

Answers

Section 2

1.
(a) (i) 3 per cent; (ii) 2 per cent. (2 marks)
(b) (i) plants; (ii) herbivores and carnivores. (2 marks)

(c) 37 per cent of energy received is lost in respiration.
37 per cent of 200 kJ = 74 kJ.   (2 marks)

2.
(a)   (i) carbon dioxide, CO_2
      (ii) starch or cellulose
      (iii) glucose, galactose or fructose
      (iv) glycogen
      (v) glucose, galactose or fructose.   (5 marks)
(b) Respiration.   (1 mark)
(c) The carbon cycle.   (1 mark)

3.
(a) Evaporation from water bodies (sea and lakes).
(b) Water from respiration.
(c) Transpiration.
(d) Evaporation from soil.
(e) Water vapour in clouds.
(f) Rain (precipitation).
(g) Rain falling on hills forms streams.
(h) River flows into sea.   (8 marks)

4.
(a) = hawk
(b) = sparrow
(c) = seeds.   (3 marks)

5.
(a) A   (b) C   (1 mark each)
(c) Primary consumers – any two of these – mice, rabbits, insects.
    Secondary consumers – any two of these – insect-eating birds, hawk,
    fox, shrew.   (2 marks)
(d) Plants → insects → insect-eating birds → hawk.   (1 mark)
(e) Respiration, transpiration, waste products.   (Any one – 1 mark)
(f) Decomposers.   (1 mark)
(g) If the rabbits were removed there would be more food available for
    other primary consumers such as mice and insects. Foxes and hawks
    would look for alternative food and would therefore eat more mice and
    birds.   (2 marks)

6.
(a) Mineral particles, water, air, mineral salts, humus, soil organisms.
                                            (3 marks – $\frac{1}{2}$ each)

(b) To find the water content of soil, first weigh it, then heat it to 100 °C to evaporate the water. After several hours, reweigh the soil. The difference in weight indicates the original water content of the soil.

(2 marks)

(c) 20 g of soil contains 5 g of water; therefore one-quarter of the soil was water. The water content of the soil was 25 per cent.

(1 mark)

(d) Sandy soils do not retain water for very long and consequently dissolved minerals are washed away faster. This can be improved by adding peat or manure to form humus. (4 marks)

7. As the numbers of species A increase, more food is available for species B. As a result, species B increases in number. Eventually there are so many of species B that there are not enough of species A to feed them all. The numbers of species B then falls due to a shortage of food. As this happens, fewer of species A are being eaten so their numbers increase again. As the numbers of species A increase, species B has more food so its numbers again increase and the cycle repeats itself.

(2 marks)

Section 3

1.
(a) If B was wiped out, more C would be eaten. At the same time, there would be more A available for C to eat. (2 marks)
(b) If C was removed from the food web, F would eat more of D, B and E. (1 mark)

2.
(a) carbon dioxide, CO_2
(b) respiration
(c) photosynthesis
(d) fossil fuels. (4 marks)

3.
(a)

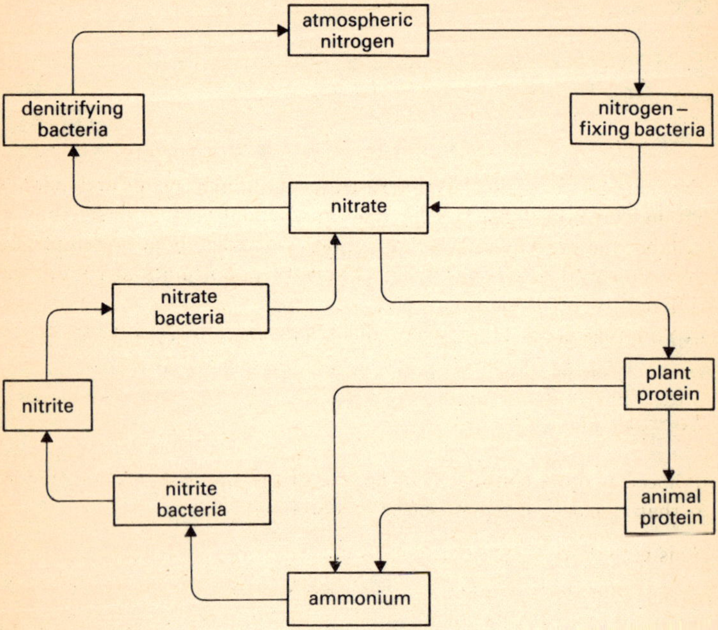

```
                         ┌──────────────┐
               ┌────────→│ atmospheric  │──────────┐
               │         │  nitrogen    │          │
               │         └──────────────┘          ↓
        ┌──────────────┐                   ┌──────────────┐
        │ denitrifying │                   │  nitrogen –  │
        │  bacteria    │                   │fixing bacteria│
        └──────────────┘                   └──────────────┘
               ↑         ┌──────────────┐          │
               └─────────│   nitrate    │←─────────┘
                         └──────────────┘
                          ↑        │
        ┌──────────────┐           │
        │   nitrate    │←──────────┘
        │  bacteria    │
        └──────────────┘
          ↑                              ┌──────────────┐
 ┌────────────┐                          │    plant     │
 │  nitrite   │                          │   protein    │
 └────────────┘                          └──────────────┘
          ↑                                      │
 ┌──────────────┐                         ┌──────────────┐
 │   nitrite    │                         │    animal    │
 │  bacteria    │                         │   protein    │
 └──────────────┘                         └──────────────┘
          ↑        ┌──────────────┐
          └────────│  ammonium    │
                   └──────────────┘
```

Fig. 13.10.   (9 marks)

(b) Clover is a leguminous plant and has root nodules containing nitrogen-fixing bacteria. This provides a source of nitrate to the soil.
(1 mark)

4.

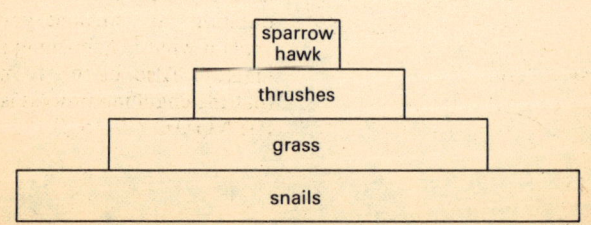

Fig. 13.11.   (3 marks)

14. The Diversity of Life

Diversity of life means that there are lots of different plants and animals around. The ones that you have to know about vary from syllabus to syllabus but the ways in which questions are asked about organisms are very similar. This chapter will give you the opportunity to try out the different types of question.

You must check to see what your syllabus requires you to know.

Section 1

Amoeba is often considered to be one of the simplest forms of life so perhaps *Amoeba* is a good place to start.

This is the sort of question you could get:

QUESTION

1. (a) with the aid of labelled diagrams explain how *Amoeba* feeds. (14 marks)

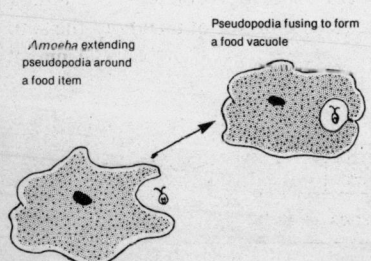
Amoeba extending pseudopodia around a food item

Pseudopodia fusing to form a food vacuole

Fig. 14.1.

COMMENT

The first thing to notice about the question is how the marks are allocated. This is a guide to how much time to spend on each section.

Part (a) has the most marks, so this is where you should concentrate your effort. You MUST use labelled diagrams because the question says so, and you must explain what is happening in each diagram. Also, be sure to mention that the engulfing process is called PHAGOCYTOSIS.

(b) What is the function of the contractile vacuole in *Amoeba*?
(4 marks)

Water enters the Amoeba *by osmosis because the cytoplasm is a stronger solution (hypertonic) than the surrounding water. The contractile vacuole fills with water before contracting to expel this excess water. This requires energy.*

If this question had just one mark allocated to it, you could answer something like 'to remove excess water'. For four marks, however, you have to do a bit more.

(c) Amoeba reproduces asexually. Name one plant and one other animal that also reproduces asexually.   (2 marks)

Plant – Mucor; *animal* – Hydra.

You just have to mention the appropriate plant and animal here.

Other possible plants are *Chlamydomonas*, *Spirogyra* or *Phytophthora*. Animals could be any other protozoan or coelenterate.

Section 2

This section, and Section 3, may contain questions on subjects that are not in your syllabus. Remember to check what you need to know before panicking about what you don't know

1. Which of the following best describes the life cycle of a fly?
   A. Egg → nymph → larva → adult.
   B. Egg → larva → pupa → adult.
   C. Egg → nymph → adult.
   D. Egg → larva → adult.   (1 mark)

2. All adult insects possess
   A. wings
   B. two pairs of antennae
   C. a chitinous exoskeleton
   D. ovipositors.   (1 mark)

3. Tapeworms and earthworms are both
   A. saprophytes
   B. hermaphrodite
   C. parasites
   D. Platyhelminthes   (1 mark)

4. The table on p. 166 shows some of the features of eight animals, A–H. From the information given, work out which major group each animal belongs to. State your reasons.   (16 marks)

5. Part of the twig of a horse chestnut tree is shown in Fig. 14.2.

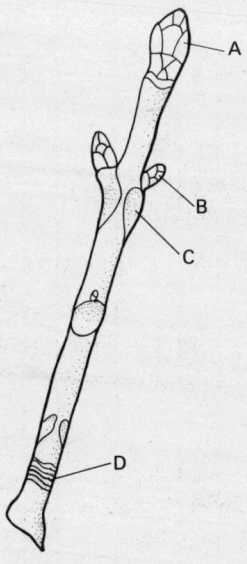

Fig. 14.2.

(a) Name parts A, B, C and D.   (4 marks)
(b) At what time of year would you expect to find such a twig?
                                                            (1 mark)
(c) Part A is sticky on the outside. Why do you think this is? (1 mark)
(d) How many years growth are shown above part D? How do you
     know?   (2 marks)

6. Figure 14.3 shows six European mammals, A–F.
If you had to identify these mammals you might use a key like the one shown in Fig. 14.4.

Feature	Animal							
	A	B	C	D	E	F	G	H
Number of wings	2	4	0	0	0	0	0	0
Number of eyes	2	2	8	2	2	0	2	Many
Number of legs	2	6	8	4	4	0	0	Many
Skeleton	Internal	External	External	Internal	Internal	Hydrostatic	Internal	External
Texture of outer surface	Feathers and scales	Hairy	Hairy	Smooth and moist	Hairy	Smooth and slimy	Dry with scales	Smooth and hard
Number of antennae	0	2	0	0	0	0	0	2
Fertilization	Internal	Internal	Internal	External	Internal	Internal	Internal	Internal
Other distinctive features	Lay eggs with hard shells	Body divided into segment	Silk produced by glands on abdomen	Breed in water. Young metamorphose into adult	Young born live and fed with milk	Body segmented	Lays eggs with leathery shells	Segmented body. Two pairs of legs per segment

(a)

(b) wing membrane

(c)

(d)

(e)

(f)

Fig. 14.3.

Use the key to identify animals A–F. (6 marks)

7. Describe four differences between a single-celled alga and a bacterium. (4 marks)

8. Figure 14.5 shows the contents of a bird's egg.

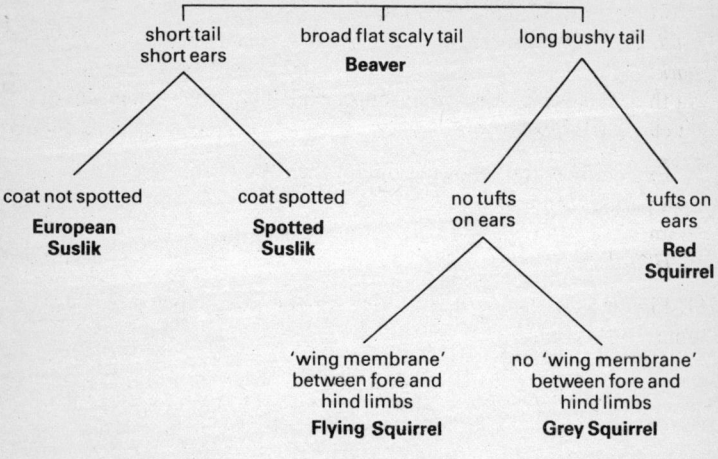

Fig. 14.4.

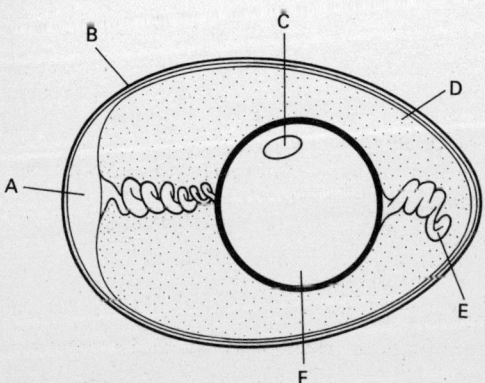

Fig. 14.5.

(a) Name the parts labelled A–F.   (6 marks)
(b) How does the developing embryo obtain its oxygen?   (2 marks)

9. The ten animals listed below can be arranged into two groups of five according to their characteristics.

Toad, fly, cockroach, cow, crab, sparrow, snake, scorpion, centipede, shark.

Put the animals into their two groups, explaining why each group of five are classified together. (2 marks)

10. Explain how the following obtain their food:
(a) a parasitic fungus
(b) an earthworm
(c) *Hydra*. (6 marks)

11. Figure 14.6 shows the life cycle of the pork tapeworm, although some words are missing.

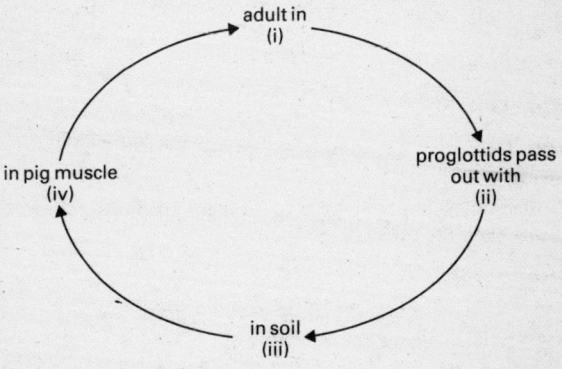

Fig. 14.6.

(a) Give appropriate terms for (i)–(iv). (4 marks)
(b) How does the structure and life cycle of the tapeworm suit its parasitic mode of life? (11 marks)

12. A pin mould, *Mucor*, is shown in Fig. 14.7.
(a) Name parts A, B and C. (3 marks)
(b) How does *Mucor* feed? (3 marks)
(c) Name a substrate on which *Mucor* might be found. (1 mark)

There are 75 marks for Section 2. Give yourself one merit mark for getting over 60, 2 merits for getting over 65.

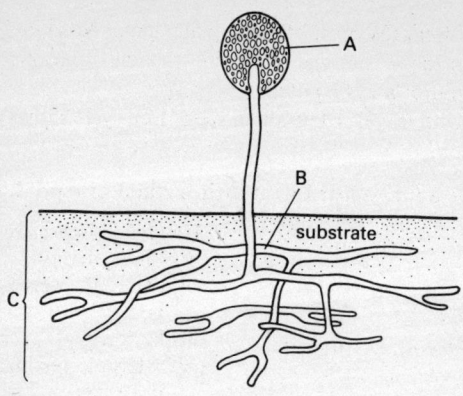

Fig. 14.7.

Section 3

Only 5 questions, but you have quite a lot to do so allow yourself 60 minutes to earn the 50 marks.

1.
(a) Draw a labelled diagram of one cell of *Spirogyra*.   (8 marks)
(b) Describe how *Spirogyra* reproduces.   (3 marks)
(c) If a cell of *Spirogyra* were tested for the presence of starch, which parts would you expect to show a positive result?   (1 mark)

2.
(a) Make a large, labelled diagram to show the external features of an insect.   (10 marks)
(b) Describe, briefly, the two main types of life cycle shown by insects, giving a named example of each.   (9 marks)
(c) Name ONE insect that is harmful to man and ONE insect that is helpful to man. State how each is either harmful or helpful.

          (4 marks)

3. Three plants are described below. Name the PHYLUM to which each belongs.

   A. Plant made of cells joined end-to-end. Each cell has spirally coiled chloroplasts. Sexual reproduction by conjugation.

B. Plant of microscopic, branching filaments. No chlorophyll present, feeds on dead organic material. Sexual reproduction leads to production of a zygospore.

C. Plant with leaves, roots and a stem. Life cycle shows alternation of generations. (3 marks)

4. Match the animals listed with their method of reproduction.

Animals	*Method of Reproduction*
A. frog	(i) binary fission
B. rabbit	(ii) external fertilization, eggs laid
C. *Amoeba*	
D. blackbird	(iii) budding
E. *Hydra*	(iv) internal fertilization, young born live
	(v) internal fertilization, eggs laid.

(5 marks)

5.
(a) Describe three ways in which bacteria can be useful to man.
(3 marks)
(b) LIST four methods of preserving food. (4 marks)
(c) Name three methods of ensuring that the food we eat does not contain live bacteria. (3 marks)

Answers

Section 2

1. B   2. C   3. B   (1 mark each)

4.
A. Bird – characterized by feathers and hard shell on eggs. (2 marks)
B. Insect – external skeleton suggests arthropod; wings and six legs indicates insect. (2 marks)
C. Spider – exoskeleton suggests arthropod; eight legs indicates arachnid; silk production suggests spider. (2 marks)
D. Amphibian – internal skeleton suggests vertebrate; metamorphosis characteristic of amphibians. (2 marks)
E. Mammal – vertebrate because of internal skeleton; presence of hair and milk characteristic of mammals. (2 marks)

F. Annelid (true worm) – characterized by smooth, slimy, segmented body with hydrostatic skeleton. (2 marks)
G. Reptile – internal skeleton, dry scaly skin, eggs with leathery shells. NOTE – no legs suggests snake, *but* there are lizards that have no legs, e.g. slow worm. (2 marks)
H. Millipede – exoskeleton suggests arthropod; two antennae and many legs indicates a myriapod; 2 pairs of legs per segment characteristic of millipedes. (2 marks)

(TOTAL = 16 marks)

5.
(a) A. terminal bud
   B. lateral bud
   C. leaf scar
   D. girdle scar (or site of last year's terminal bud). (4 marks)
(b) Winter. (1 mark)
(c) To prevent water loss. (1 mark)
(d) One year's growth, because there are no more girdle scars between D and the terminal bud. (2 marks)

6.
A. grey squirrel
B. flying squirrel
C. red squirrel
D. European suslik
E. spotted suslik
F. beaver. (6 marks)

7. Algae have chlorophyll in chloroplasts. Those bacteria that do contain chlorophyll have it scattered in the cytoplasm; it is not found in chloroplasts.

Nuclear material in algae is contained in the nucleus. In bacteria it is loose in the cytoplasm.

The cell wall in bacteria is made of fat and protein; in algae it is made of cellulose.

Algae have membrane-bound organelles in the cytoplasm; bacteria do not. (4 marks)

8.
(a) A. air space
   B. shell
   C. embryo (or germinal disc)
   D. albumen

    E. chalaza
    F. yolk.   (6 marks)
(b) Oxygen from the surrounding air diffuses through pores in the shell
    into the air space. From there it diffuses through the albumen and
    yolk to the embryo. As the embryo grows a network of capillaries
    develops to absorb oxygen over a greater surface area.   (2 marks)

9.
Group 1 – toad, cow, sparrow, snake, shark – all vertebrates.
                                                          (1 mark)
Group 2 – fly, cockroach, crab, scorpion, centipede – all invertebrates;
    also, all arthropods.   (1 mark)

10.
(a) Digestive enzymes are secreted which enter and break down the cells
    of the host. The digested products are then absorbed into the
    fungus.   (2 marks)
(b) Earthworms take in vegetation and soil particles through the mouth.
    Food substances are digested by enzymes in the gut and the products
    are absorbed.   (2 marks)
(c) Small organisms are paralysed by sting cells and delivered to the
    mouth by the tentacles. They are partly digested by enzymes in the
    enteron. Particles are ingested by phagocytosis into nutritive cells
    which complete the digestive process.   (2 marks)

11.
(a)   (i) human gut
     (ii) faeces
    (iii) embryo
     (iv) bladderworm.   (4 marks)
(b) This can be answered in essay form or as a list. You should mention
these points:
    Structural adaptations
        (i) Scolex has hooks and suckers for secure attachment to host's
            gut.
       (ii) Muscles are poorly developed as little movement is required.
      (iii) There are no sense organs as these are not required.
       (iv) A thick cuticle prevents the tapeworm being digested by the
            host's enzymes.
    Feeding adaptations
        (v) There is no digestive system as the food has already been
            digested by the host.

(vi) The body is flattened to increase the surface area for absorption of digested food.

Physiological adaptations

(vii) There is no oxygen in the human gut so tapeworms respire anaerobically.

Reproductive adaptations

(viii) Tapeworms are unlikely to meet other tapeworms so they are hermaphrodite and produce eggs by self-fertilization.

(ix) Many eggs are produced to increase the chances of some of them being ingested by the secondary host.

(x) Eggs may have to remain in the soil for a long time before being ingested by a secondary host. They are therefore very resistant to adverse conditions.

(xi) Use of a secondary host which is eaten by the primary host increases the chance of the life cycle being completed.

(11 marks)
(1 for each point)

12.

(a) A. sporangium
B. hypha
C. mycelium. (3 marks)

(b) Mucor is a saprophyte. Digestive enzymes are secreted on to the substrate. The products of digestion are absorbed into the hyphae.

(3 marks)

(c) This could be any moist food, such as damp bread. (1 mark)

Section 3

1.

(a)

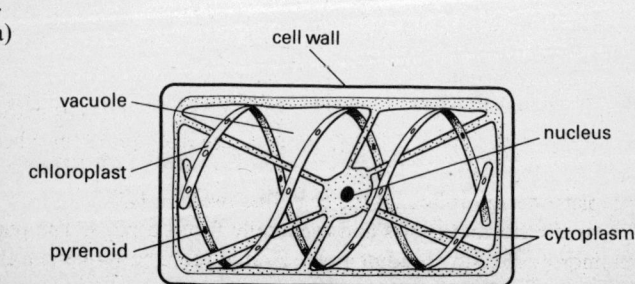

Fig. 14.8.   (8 marks)
(2 for accurate diagram, 6 for labels)

(b) Spirogyra reproduces both sexually and asexually. Asexual reproduction is by binary fission, forming a long filament of cells. Sexual reproduction is by conjugation, where the cell contents of two adjacent filaments mix and the nuclei fuse. Conjugation results in a zygospore. (3 marks)

NOTE. *If there were more than 3 marks allocated for (b) you would have to go into more detail about conjugation.*

(c) Around the pyrenoids. (1 mark)

2.

(a)

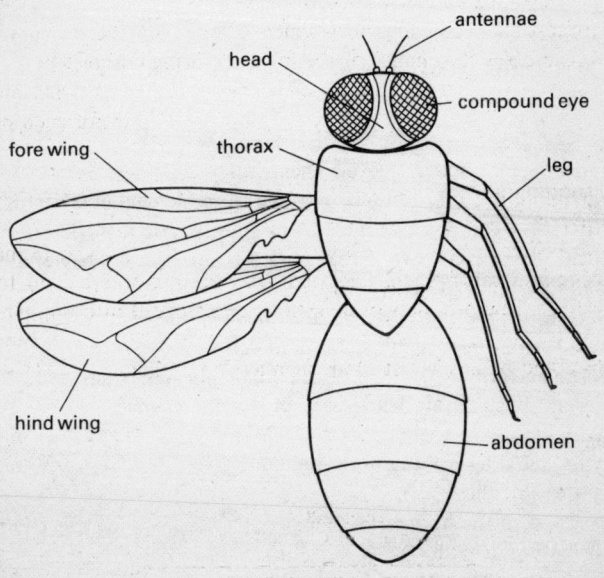

Fig. 14.9. (10 marks)
(2 for accurate diagram, 8 for labels)

(b) Complete metamorphosis – the egg gives rise to a larva.
The larva feeds and grows and eventually forms a pupa. The pupa metamorphoses into the adult insect. Examples are butterflies, moths, flies.
Incomplete metamorphosis – from the egg hatches a nymph. The nymph feeds and grows, going through a series of stages or instars.

The instars resemble the adult except that they do not have wings and are not sexually mature. The final moult leads to the adult which has wings and fully developed sex organs. Examples are cockroach, locust.   (9 marks)

(c) There are many possible answers here. The most obvious are perhaps the mosquito as a harmful insect because it spreads malaria and the honey bee because it pollinates our plants and also produces honey.

3.
A. Algae
B. Fungi
C. Pteridophyta (fern).   (3 marks)

4.
A with (ii); B with (iv); C with (i); D with (v); E with (iii).   (5 marks)

5.
(a) Any 3 of these:
   – Saprophytic bacteria recycle chemicals.
   – Nitrifying bacteria produce nitrates from nitrogenous wastes.
   – Nitrogen fixers form nitrates from atmospheric nitrogen.
   – Dead organisms are broken down by decay bacteria (decomposers).
   – Bacteria in the gut of herbivores produce the enzyme cellulase to help break down cellulose in plant cell walls.
   – Some bacteria in the guts of mammals produce vitamins.
   – Certain bacteria are being used in genetic engineering.
                                                                         (3 marks)
(b) Drying, pickling, salting, freezing.   (4 marks)
(c) Any three of these:
   cleanliness in the home
   chlorinating drinking water
   pasteurizing milk
   boiling food
   pressure cooking food.   (3 marks)